praise for Mike Dockins

Dazzling and dizzying are the two words that come to mind after reading Mike Dockins' latest collection of poetry, *Letter to So-and-So from Wherever.* In this remarkable compilation of letter-poems, Dockins is a darkly comic contemporary Whitman—his language as rich and stunning, his reach as exuberant and far-ranging. From the hilariously poignant opening missive to Santa Claus to the final lines of 'Letter to Sanders from Academia'—his zany critique of (among other things) academia and corporate America—this book will carry you on a brilliant and wildly magnificent ride.

BETH GYLYS
Spot in the Dark

The thousand injuries of wasting through nearly eight years—eight years!—between books by Mike Dockins! I have grown thin and ragged. O how the insufferable suffering of the universe has screamed—no, yawped—for this. It was well worth the wait. America's book reviewers take note upon your iPads: here's the language laid brutally honest and crankified. Find and grip tiny thesauri to discover violent verbs that describe this assault: a pummeling, whomping, pugilating new collection.

JAMIE IREDELL
I Was a Fat Drunk Catholic School Insomniac

Careful, thoughtful, sometimes painful, often adventuresome, Mike Dockins' *Letter to So-and-So from Wherever* lets us in to some of the byways by which we know one another, address one another, by one of the most sacred means there is.

DARA WIER
You Good Thing

Winner of the Maxine Kumin Prize in Poetry 2013

LETTER TO SO-AND-SO FROM WHEREVER

LETTER TO SO-AND-SO FROM WHEREVER

Mike Dockins

C&R PRESS 2014

PRESS

FIRST EDITION

ISBN-13: 978-1-936196-49-4
ISBN-10: 1-936196-49-2
LCCN: 2014943297

Book interior & cover design
by Terrence Chouinard
wingwheel.com

Poems

Letter to Claus from Walnut Creek 1
Letter to Denton from O'Hare 6
Letter to Art from Greenwich 9
Letter to Johnston from Carlisle 12
Letter to Jenks from Hurricane Ivan 15
Letter to Jenks from Hurricane Jeanne 18
Letter to Gylys from Midtown 20
Letter to Moon from Luquillo 23
Letter to English 101 from the South Fucking Pole 28
Letter to Bonczek from Brockport 34
Letter to Seaton from a Little Ice Age 38
Letter to Riggs from Cobble Hill 41
Letter to Wright from Croton Point 46
Letter to Dockins from a Foreign Country 51
Letter to Iredell from the Yucatán 56
Channeling Dockins, Iredell Replies from Breadloaf 63
Letter to Li Po from Vickery's 68
Letter to Meserve from Orgeval 77
Letter to Self at 22 from 35 89
Letter to So-and-So from Wherever 94
Letter to Sanders from Academia 97

ACKNOWLEDGMENTS 105
THE POET 107
THE PRIZE 109

for Richard Hugo

All I wanted was to go somewheres.
HUCKLEBERRY FINN

We know not where we are.
HENRY DAVID THOREAU

Sometimes a scream is better than a thesis.
RALPH WALDO EMERSON

Letter to Claus from Walnut Creek

Santa, I'll buy the elves and flying ungulates.
Coleridge calls it the willful
suspension of disbelief. But as a ninja
mathematician, I've decided that delivering
toys to the world's children in one evening
is impossible.
Must all of your toy recipients be good
Christians? Can an atheist be rewarded?
How about a pious Qur'an-banger?
A Buddha-bellied disciple of the Tao?
A pine-hugging pagan?
A shaggier-than-thou Isis-thumper? How
about children beyond even the Third World—
howling at an Amazon Moon, howling
at the toyless jungle on the Moon....
Meantime, I am chimneyless.
Will you pass like a comet
over this California bungalow?
I'd sooner receive nothing than a lump
of coal. There are still places
where you can watch the long trains loosen
like dark ribbons toward the horizon,
each car balancing a tenuous meniscus
of coal that will never overspill.
Are these trains bound for the North Pole?
As a boy, I'd count cars with my dad,
out on the dusty Great Plains where the sky
yawns its desolation all the way to Beijing.
I learned infinity
from my dad, his face buried

in astronomy journals—milky spirals
reflected in his spectacles as he spoke the Word:
billion. I'd drift under the tide
of sleep, the word humming
against the knots of my spine: *billion,*
the word multiplying in the riverine
grooves of my brain.
Santa, a billion children romp this Earth,
and more spring up every season.
Soon the planet will be a vast sandbox,
a single colossal tire swing
arcing like a pendulum over a bottomless pond
that ripples with my dad's voice: *trillion,*
quadrillion, quintillion, sextillion, septillion,
octillion, nonillion, decillion. . . .
Santa, I'm dizzy.
Is this how you feel when you sail
under the rooftop of the world, the endless *illions*
stinging you with pins of light?
I take it back—I don't buy the flying reindeer.
O childhood is a cornucopia
of lies, a ribboned box of hyperbole:
your reindeer fly simply by rowing the air,
pawing the stratosphere, hoofing
barbaric yawps across the icicled evening?
I lack such a ninja mojo for physics,
but what about friction?
Me = perplexed, O algebraic bewilderment.
Isaac Newton rolls in his toyless grave. . . .
Ah, but the utility of an elf: slave labor

is rampant in southeast Asia,
and, by god, America shall have six-dollar jerseys
and blinking Nikes....
Crap, now I'm sure to get coal.
But I offer you this humble sack
of honesty, and my list is not unreasonable.
Example: clementine oranges.
They're in season, and Spain is bursting
with them: clementines in knapsacks,
clementines rolling down Gothic alleyways,
clementines spilling from taxicabs....
What I want is eclectic,
yet you hang out in shopping malls,
those cradles of misery. Fuck misery.
Have you ever been in a Baptist church?
The joy in there travels forever—
an ant crawling a möbius, its thorax
strumming infinity, and the ant singing
a buggy little hymn to endlessness....
But this bungalow is no church.
When my tribe of heathens crouches
round the fake pine festooned with brittle planets,
do you think we're thinking of the little baby
Jesus? We're lucky if we're not hungover.
Curses, we're all aging,
and the holidays have become an odyssey
of brain-sizzling, sky-scraping, sleigh-smashing,
gin-swigging oblivion. Santa, I hang over
my thirties like a hummingbird.
But I was once a toddler, and I caught my mom

wrapping a green stuffed puppy
as carols squeaked from a cheap phonograph—
Burl Ives, Mitch Miller, Mahalia Jackson:
snowflakes and the little baby Jesus
swimming in the grooves of a 78, swimming
that circle like a vinyl comet
lapping a vinyl star. It's a starless
evening in the Bay Area, and typically foggy.
How can a single red nose glow (like a light
bulb!) through such nebulous nebulae?
I doubt that 'White Christmas' was a big hit
in these fogbound towns, Mount Diablo looming
snowless and still.
I grew up where it snows and snows.
And way upstate from there,
82 inches have fallen across five days:
a cloud the size of Lake Erie mushrooms over Buffalo.
It's a fabled nuclear winter—treacherous
ashes settle upon oak branches and landfills,
upon stranded schoolbuses and tenement sills.
The snow-day index spoils the Buffalo
schoolchildren: they'll grow old, never know
what it's like to suffer. Santa,
I've run out of grandparents.
The last one died at 100.
Even her pacemaker was older than me.
And I think she was made of wheat.
Wheat and rhubarb. Wheat and rhubarb
and wind. A Nebraska pioneer gal, she'd saved
bags by the bag-load. My dad

has inherited these *illion* bags—infinite space
waiting to be filled. He should ship them
to Buffalo. Seven feet, Santa.
The Great Lakes are merciless:
bags and bags and bags and bags
of water. The polar wind rakes across them,
peels helpless faces like oranges....
And here, tonight, I'll wait for the California sky
to turn orange—clementines
parachuting like snowflakes, or bombs:
the gift of seeds, of pulp, of acid,
the gift of skin—
because soon enough I'll be a sack of bones
slouching in a titanic steel sleigh
pulled by what physics I can't imagine,
and praying to sweet nothing
that the wings will hold, that the engines
will not fall to the cracked earth,
and that the wheels will open like rose petals
above a runway sprawling toward home.

Letter to Denton from O'Hare

Travis, the skyline is oscillating.
The chapels are exhausted:
thousands of 'Just Married' limousines
drag skillets and jumper cables
all the way to Indiana, clatter
toward the smokestacks pulsing like cannons,
belching existentialism
into a Midwestern sky the color of motor oil.
Dude, my cells are multiplying—
I can hear them. Like children
strung out on gumdrops and Oreos,
they count to infinity, and again....
I scrape crushed empires from the bottom
of my sneakers: luminous streaks
on the sidewalk like the guts of fireflies.
Last night the sky over Lake Michigan
was a luminous splash of static fireflies
trapped in the cosmic fishing nets,
but nevertheless pulsing,
the way wasps in autumn say *fuck it*
through the first swarm of snowflakes—
or through the swarm of atoms leaping
from the season's first flake—
then crawl the dark, waspy miles
into the honeycomb's sublime tremors,
slinging prayers from rickety thoraxes
for a safe cocoon, a place to harvest
the next millennium of baby wasps,
dreaming of spilled root beer and picnic stings....
This morning I watch dust rise
over the city as on every corner stadiums

implode to make room for coconut trees
whose leaves don't sway in the wind
off Lake Michigan because, by god,
coconut trees will not be juggled with.
Tonight they will silhouette the Moon,
and the Moon will continue to howl
at poets ankle-deep in a rubble of jet engines.
You've climbed your mailbox, T,
even this very Sunday—King of Grant Park,
legs dangling like Tom Sawyer—
a-fishin' for hieroglyphic pebbles:
how rare, how prehistoric, how pharaohic....
Your little biscuit of a dog
wishes she were a hound, something meatier
to bark away the sour news seething
like rabies inside the crates and crates
of self-addressed envelopes.
When the dark fleet of mail trucks
spills down Hill Street in treacherous spirals,
you have to wipe away the spittle and foam,
and that's when the tequila worm skewered
on your fish hook wriggles off,
muttering *fuck it*
to your lawn's late-March detritus blustering
round and round your urban bungalow
like cluster-bomb shrapnel
celebrating a job well done
in a country nobody can spell....
Now, uncork the cigars, set a match
to the lip of a wine bottle,
and stare directly into the sun,

and soon you will spot Isaac Newton
sporting a wife-beater, a margarita
in one hand, an apple in the other, an apple
like the first apple—O tragically flawed
Miltonian creation, O idiot Milton—
the apple shaped like a zero
pummeled and pummeled, Newton
sucking beads of calculus from his salty wrists,
explaining gravity to the lime pulp....
Dude, fuck it.
The skyline oscillates back home, too.
When the Republicans die
of starvation, when the spy satellites drop
from the Moon to rust in the gator swamp,
when the stadiums un-implode and fill back up
with beer cans and ballcaps,
that's when Atlantis will at last be discovered—
in the Great Barrier Reef,
under the Polynesian batholith,
under miles of Antarctic ice—
Atlantis in its ancient honeycomb tomb.
Archaeologists will find it teeming with moss:
moss on its temples,
moss in its lungs, moss on its arthritic knuckles,
and a scrim of moss scrimming a new horizon
along each rib, a new horizon
spotted inside a telescope lens, dark with volcano
or coconut tree or seagull,
and god-dammit all to hell, Travis,
we're going to raise our sails.

Letter to Art from Greenwich

Robyn, we've made it
out of Grand Central Station alive.
The pigeons have been eviscerated
and boxed up, and now sail
via tanker to Madagascar.
The smoothie shop has flopped.
All the street names in Manhattan
have been switched, and lost
tourists stagger across a moonscape,
their fat camera lenses shuddering
at the lips of immense craters,
the craters themselves scarred by craters....
Battery Park is littered
with batteries, and skyscrapers
loom from Central Park ponds,
their windows flush with algae
and with the terrified breath
of tie-choked suckers trapped inside.
Even the ragged Bryant Park chess champions
sport 401Ks while you and I hover
over idle typewriter keys and loose crumbs.
We've made it
to our respective suburbs,
but I'd rather be in Brooklyn,
or even my dilapidated, rotten hometown.
Meantime, Greenwich is peppered
with a surprising number of rednecks
who chop down every possible tree
and green plant, who waddle by their pools,
and who round the clock howl

at their huskies and hounds to stop howling.
Robyn, all creatures were born howling,
and we haven't stopped.
Even the lifeless protons
in my tropical pineapple shirt
howl with a desire I can't fathom,
some cottony impossibility.
Worse, the second-hand won't stop
howling for the next second,
confirming the non-existence
of the present moment, of a *now*.
Remember when we met under the big clock?
Seems like two days ago, and it was—
already I'm brimming with nostalgia
for train engines screeching
to a halt in the tunnels, grinding molecules
of god-knows-what elements, the echoes
bouncing between the stars
scrawled on the station ceiling,
the constellations playing sonic volleyball....
Long-winded, but the suburbs are a bore
without you—your hair clips,
your lipstick, your tattoos.
I've discovered that I still have ten toes,
ten fingers, and that my thumbs have lost
no capacity to twiddle, O Atari childhood,
O pixeled imagination. My imagination,
that soup pot, begins to seethe:
a multitude of Robyn Arts
teems inside your typewriter—

they scamper across the flimsy ribbon,
little bioluminescent Robyn Arts
igniting the keys. Is this blinding?
Do the keys melt as you strike them?
Your hands trace microcosmic ellipses.
My hands trace microcosmic ellipses.
Around what star do they tumble and spin?
We're both waiting for that comet, aren't we,
slouching like teenagers in its path.
I say: Bring it on. Or: Let's roll.
Yes, let's evoke that trumped-up heroism
at the Apocalypse, and we'll roll together
off the planet when it's hit. At last, Robyn,
an unignorable *now:* billions of smashed clocks,
our pupils wider than the dark
hole in the Earth—we who had never seen
such divine art.

Letter to Johnston from Carlisle

Audrey, the cicadas are still
threatening to leap in ragged clusters
from poplar leaves and spit pestilence
upon this truck-choked town.
Here is their sinister crescendo—
their voices thrumming with chlorophyll,
with a staccato ill will.
I'll keep a fifth eye on them—
their trail of shells, of brittle wings,
of black eyes like the husks of dead planets.
The sidewalks pulse, but that's only the ripple
from beefed-up cars ripping High Street
to dismal shreds of tar and oil
and crumbs of taillight.
Thunderstorms lunge across campus
like teenagers slamming doors
on spent childhoods, gasping arias
from tattered lungs.
This town is a factory of noise,
a jackhammer jackhammering inside a proton—
out, out, out—
the first ordinary grasshopper's brain
to turn black and crackle.
The cicadas might think they're locusts,
as everybody else does, so I'll bolt
my door, stand vigil until dawn gripping
a baseball bat, a skillet, a floury rolling pin,
my bathrobe flowing, curlers in my hair....
I'll rattle inside my sneakers.
Even the menacing spider—

her web slung taut to catch the cosmos—
trembles at the center, noiseless
and patient, a tiny black hole.
For three weeks you skated on spiderweb,
your spiral notebook cocooned in metaphors:
what will emerge?
By now you've settled back into home,
and bend like a riverbank around hills
old and slow as local barbers. I hope
you're bending verbs, mauling adjectives,
twisting their thumbs until the words cry *uncle*.
I hope your pencil is free of termites, that it draws
hieroglyphs from your blood like a mosquito.
I hope it hurts—this is the only way
we re-invent ourselves, our old skin molted and tossed.
All our lives we lift pillows and something rolls away:
a quarter shiny as hope.
Hope hope hope hope hope.
And I hope the New England silence is splintered
only by the snap of balled-up paper,
that your room is a clutter of these crumpled moons.
Audrey, were you born on the Moon,
from one of the ancient lunar wombs
which we don't even need a telescope to see?
Did you simply spill to Earth, tumble
through ionosphere, stratosphere, biosphere,
all the way to Vermont?
I wish I could say I witnessed it:
some evening at the end of high school,
the sky iced over and starless,

the Moon howling in labor—
its contractions tripling coastal tides,
its umbilicus flailing like a sine curve,
the terrible curve of motherhood
strung between horizons—and I muttered
wow from some sloppy suburb
hundreds of miles away, reaffirming
my disbelief in God.... But I missed it,
too young and dumb for the sublime.
And now, one cicada cycle later,
here in the ribcage of Pennsylvania,
I cannot tell you what to expect from this cosmos,
all the ways you will be surprised,
how you will marvel.
And, because there can be no yin without yang,
how you will weep.
Like I want to now: a single cicada
writhing in its madness, spirals of DNA
stabbing brain cells—*leap, leap, leap*—
and like a dark ship of moonlight it sails
over porch and tree and rooftop and steeple,
and is gone.

Letter to Jenks from Hurricane Ivan

Allison, you board the windows and I'll squeeze
the limes. You scrawl epithets for Ivan
in lipstick across the planks—IVAN YOU JERK,
SCREW YOU IVAN, IVAN KISS MY ASS—
and I'll lean like a hunchback over the balcony,
howling *Mai Tai! Hurricane!*—irritating
the litters of strays that slink and yowl
through this neighborhood choked
with hip nightclubs, the cats soaked
to their feline spines.
You measure wind velocity with pinwheels
and I'll close and open
the drink umbrellas, snap them
like toothpicks in my tiny wooden rage.
An old man staggers down 12th, begs
his mangled umbrella for mercy.
And it's mercy that circles him
relentlessly round the block, thick arms flailing....
Allison, have you seen the weather maps?
The isobars expand like atomic shock waves.
Not even the techies can keep up
with these god-damned isobars,
and their spectacles cloud in aggravation.
What hope do we have when our geniuses fail?
But the news writers save us, don't they,
peppering the bulletins with aggressive verbs:
IVAN POUNDS GULF COAST
IVAN BASHES MOBILE
IVAN PUMMELS PANAMA CITY
IVAN BATTERS DAUPHIN ISLAND

IVAN WALLOPS WHEREVER. . . .

Hallelujah, the news writers have emerged
from their think-tank with dog-eared thesauruses
and a Christmas list of menacing verbs
flapping in the menacing wind.
And just in time, my Sweet.
We'd been anxious the Apocalypse might skirt us,
millimeters to the east—the Apocalypse
our only salvation: our skeletons
entwined beneath shelves
and shelves of canned peas, the skeletons
of canned peas. . . .
Meantime, the techies have been straitjacketed—
tongues lolling, irises kaleidoscopic tempests—
the poor wretches muttering *Doppler*. . . .
Allison, I wish meteorology were the study of meteors.
I wish this rain were a rain of meteors slashing
a windless sky, and I would name each one *Allison*.
Say the word, *meteor*, and let me watch your mouth.
These pounding, bashing, pummeling, battering,
walloping winds only make me lonely.
So pad the basement walls
and I'll scrape muck from the blender.
You telegram a will to loved ones
and I'll dust off the megaphone
to announce the arrival of Happy Hour,
even for those emaciated strays.
You kennel the puppies and the guppies
and the Triops, and I'll hunt for a Theory
of Everything in Ivan's galactic arms.

I am suddenly in love: swirl with me.
Have you piled sandbags on the levee?
Don't worry, the city will evacuate.
Love, have you dried up from exhaustion?
Don't worry, the cabinet is full of salt.

Letter to Jenks from Hurricane Jeanne

Allison, I'm not done,
and neither is the atmosphere.
The weather geeks have cycled and recycled
through a flimsy alphabet like toddlers
screeching ABCs—irises swirling,
lungs swollen with wind.
A necklace of hurricanes beads the Atlantic.
A whip of hurricanes lashes westward:
a parade of pinwheels, a luminous belt
in the constellation of a hunter. . . .
O Allison, I am sick
of metaphor. But to be literal in a surreal world
is ludicrous. Example: *the south-*
eastern U.S. is enduring too many tropical storms.
Expository! Obvious! Dull!
I'd rather choke back bilious metaphor:
Haiti is underwater, an Atlantis of mud and straw. . . .
And Florida is a thing simply to be pitied.
Remember when Bugs Bunny sawed it off,
and the state floated away like driftwood,
like an ark? Unlikely, if one chooses to be literal—
but that's all that will save Florida now.
The palm trees are tired
of posing for news cameras, bored
by the ceaseless bending and swaying.
Even the alligators are spent, and waddle
to Albuquerque, to Pismo Beach, to the North Pole,
scale by miserable scale, tail by dismal tail. . . .
Floridians don't even watch the weather
anymore. They slog from errand to errand,

weighed down by scuba tanks,
too exhausted even to sigh as they mail packages,
sift for ripe lemons in the grocery,
walk their soaked and panicked spaniels.
They know that Killer is next,
followed by Lasher and Monster
and Nailbiter and Ogre and Punisher—
all lined up like fucking reindeer.
Allison, my poor Florida belle,
where can I keep you safe? What fabled Ark
can I rent for us, what marine limousine,
and where could we sail? Not even outer space,
Love: more spirals, cosmic hurricanes—
too many galaxies to name, and not enough
alphabets to name them. Only a gorgeous
view for us to curse, to spit beer at,
as we're lashed by solar wind,
our ship's hull pelted by rocky debris—
a stinging rain emptied of all mercy.

Letter to Gylys from Midtown

Beth, Hugo's dead and I'm 32 and still
I collect money wires from my dad who suffers
God-fearing yokels in the Nebraska
Panhandle while I suffer God-
fearing yokels in this cosmopolitan,
metro-sexual metropolis and still I own no car
or television which means I'm deprived
of reality and my refrigerator is desolate
but for three empty pizza boxes and my wallet
is a hive of moths and my wallet is thinner
than a cracker and my wallet sings
a lonesome aria and my wallet is a godless tundra
and I can afford only to wonder
where the spiders in my apartment hide
their webs throbbing with star-crossed flies....
All this, like that sentence, makes me
breathless, and I'm lucky
for my stash of bronchial puffers
because my lungs are deflated dodgeballs,
get flatter as the nanoseconds wheeze by,
because my lungs are weeds
in a godless tundra, because my lungs
choke on little empty wallets—
my dismal, dismal lungs.
Beth, it's Friday night and I'm trapped
at home, webbed like a fly in a spidery poem.
The young co-ed I've been seeing
must be sailing through my neighborhood
saloon, swimming laps in a pink martini,
waiting for me to stagger in with my storm cloud,

swatting tiny lightning bolts like mosquitoes.
I'd slouch toward her—drenched, thirsty,
wanting to lick her—but I'd never
survive the block: 12th Street is infested
with a dozen nightclubs thumping
a relentless thump, each bass note a Big Bang—
universes of infinite racket shockwaving Atlanta.
12th is jammed with jacked-up
stretch Humvees, and the sidewalks seethe
with the best minds of my generation:
Young Folks Who Look Good.
They bubble like fire ants
from those smoky dungeons, and their cells
thrum and their vapid trophy dates
beam the beam that nothingness beamed
when nothingness burst into somethingness.
To get to my Sweet, who thinks nothing
of me (it's really something), I'd have to clomp
up and down the hoods and roofs and trunks
of parked cars, only to get pummeled
by some jarhead douchebag showing off for his skank
because I smudged his SUV with my flimsy sneakers.
So I'll stay at home and sing to the spiders,
make out with my imagination,
fuck my imagination
senseless. And this is just to say
thanks for being my #1 fan.
I feel like the lovable Doctor Carlos
having swiped some icebox plums and scrawling
a missive to Flossie on a colossal Sticky-Note.

So much to say: tectonic continents
of nouns, seething galaxies of verbs,
and I'm covered with Sticky-Notes,
and my pens and pencils kick the can-can,
a taunting chorus line—but this is all the love
I'll get tonight, except that I'm thankful
to have even one fan because I can recall
a time when I was fanless:
months of small-town belly-aching
and a trashcan bubbling over with atrocious poems,
and I could barely afford all that paper
I crumpled.
Sestinas? Villanelles? I could barely tie my shoes,
could barely piss straight on an alley wall
after a good beer-soak,
and again this breathlessness—my lungs
picket for a cleaner city, some city
that starves for a nightclub,
some town whose only sound
is crickets combing the thickets,
a hamlet of existential citizens,
a sleepy village illuminated
by ten billion constellations.
Beth, there is no such city. But in that city
an aloof and sexy co-ed, some Elizabeth,
waits for me to call a third, a fourth,
a billionth time—asking me,
begging me, to lick her.

Letter to Moon from Luquillo

Moon, the Moon is swollen: a little
Moon baby inside fins through lunar amnion.
The Earth suffers an extra tugging, the violent
kick of tides. Hanging like a lamp
over the Atlantic, the Moon's a skeleton
of an unblinking eye, a luminous fossil:
flakes of light scatter and settle.
Rungs of moonlight on the water climb north—
to the horizon, to winter: No thanks.
Now that I've buried you
under a pile of metaphors, listen as I ring
in your holiday season: *Feliz Navidad, Amigo,*
from your old hometown—beaches strung
with seaweed and *gringos,*
the elusive *coquí* piping nocturnes
from dark limbs, twelve-foot waves
menacing rookie swimmers, the silence
of reefs, and, beyond this rented condo,
the jungled, lusty peaks of *El Yunque.*
A happy nativity, indeed.
Hell, praise
even the senseless drivers here.
Laneless (it would appear), brainless
(ditto), they constantly risk absurdity and death:
every nanosecond, they avoid wrecks
by the thinnest nanometers,
and, when they fail, flecks of busted taillight
reflect and refract fragments of Moon,
which tonight will be no less full as it hums
in Spanish to the coconut trees.

I love how even humming is Spanish here.
The view from this balcony is not darkened
by snow and ice: no bus-stop slush blackened
by exhaust, no snow-bent pines
pining for July, no jolly
corn-cob-piped snowmen, no angels
winged onto lawns, no icicled sedans
plowed into suburban curbs by civic bureaucrats....
The view is a postcard—
from where else but Elsewhere?—
stamped with exotic ink and a note scribbled
by a jackass friend who gloats:
I'm not coming back, suckers.
And I might not, Tony—not even
to slouch over the good old bar,
my daily swim in a mug of PBR.
Plenty of *cerveza* here, and a hammock
filled with limes. Curse my obsession with limes!
Lime lime lime lime lime.
My brain is pulp.
O I shall never be tangled in the vines
of scurvy! It's a Citrus Moon, Moon—
a wedge of lime
leaping the leapable tropics.
One more rum-and-pineapple (with lime)
and I'll be Li Po, swatting at the Moon
as it paces Orion, Orion
swinging from his ancient trapeze, his sword—
no, fuck it, his machete—
hacking cosmic jungle: vines of stars, infinite

vines like seaweed, thrumming with stars.
Curses, there I go again trying to make it
matter that I'm alive, that my subatomic little self
is worth one quarky iota
despite the vast and empty and lifeless
light-years. But the roar of surf carries me
back to The Beginning: loose atoms
gathering, singing me into me, singing,
'Let's be the illustrious Mike Dockins.'
Praise the womb—that first hammock!
O to be marooned on *la isla bonita*
the way we're all marooned in space,
though this fact is never a source of marvel
for our fellow Earthlings—
thanks be to Sony, to MTV,
thanks be to the great starless cities of this world,
the titanic incandescent bulb
into which the planet is ever evolving....
To gather coconuts while I may,
until I die!—my arteries stunned
by leisure. To write poems about gathering
coconuts until a coconut I become, and lose
all sense.... In other words, I wish
not to go back: to stale bibliographies,
to freshmen stoned on weed,
stoned on boredom, stoned on Nintendo,
back to butchered sentences and dismal words,
back to swarms of ragged hobos
lined up outside my window—tin cups rattling
sad little death-rattles—back to jammed

subway cars denser than the universe
one nanosecond before the Big Bang (O theory),
or back to my cobwebbed mailbox (O reality)....
I'll stay here with my brothers—a century
of living among us—and all of us scheming:
how, without disaster, to hurl
beer bottles into the pool from this behammocked
balcony—what a marvelous arc
to behold, the segment of what delirious orbit?
And such sublime laziness!—we're stretching
what youth may still cling to our ribs
(that cage), what youth may still ride the surf
of each cell.... Ah, Youth: our thirties roar,
vanish like sea spray, like Moon dust.
Tony, pal of pals, may you strike the lucky
Powerball, fix your rusted muffler, retire
to a Luquillo bungalow made of gold and C-notes.
May you receive Purple Hearts unwounded, far
from the pawns of some clown's capricious war.
And may you meet, at Vickery's, septets
more stunning than the Pleiades, and may they cluster
round you—a harem, amen.
But don't be greedy, you hound—save one
for me so that I may retire with her
to some remote rock, some moon, uncluttered
by televisions, worthless
(sophomoric!) freshman essays, the sadness
of empty spaces in this universe,
the sadness of empty souls. Moon, god-dammit,
did I just say *soul?*—O I shall stagger

willingly to the gallows.... The Soul,
like Time, may not exist. Depends
on what you believe. I believe in synapses
firing at random, and in the rising Moon: fuller
than full, several months along—too many
to count or fathom—and, any minute now,
expecting.

Letter to English 101 from the South Fucking Pole

This is a good page.
It is blank,
And getting blanker.
LARRY LEVIS

Class, let's celebrate the loss
of another calendar,
crumpled like a dismal essay draft
in a trashcan that is itself
crumpled and dismal. Happy New Year.
Hallelujah, I resolve to abstain
from the wine of metaphor: everything
I say shall be journalistic and literal,
and I shall report all events exactly
as they happen. Example: *The stars*
are a many-necked necklace.
Crap, I'm a failure.
The sky over Atlanta is almost pointless,
literally: three, maybe four stars,
the stubborn ones, dying
to stir any of you into what
my old mentor calls a long stare. If only
you could be dwarfed yet heartened
by the night sky over Valentine,
Nebraska—miles and miles
from any star-dissolving metropolis,
and from whence is visible
the entire cosmos, the Milky Way
swaying like a hammock over the Great Plains.
Class, in Valentine the cosmos sings.
If only you could listen to each holy eon.

And while you're looking up
eon, let me tell you a bedtime story.
Not so long ago, in this very galaxy,
I heard one of your peers debating whether
or not to take Astronomy: he thought
he would 'look at clouds and shit.'
The End.
And don't try to tell me that he was thinking
cosmic nebulae, i.e. Horseshoe, i.e. Orion,
i.e. Crab.
O the abyss will swallow him
and not even bother to spit out his skeleton
if he fails to discover the Grand
Canyon of himself—the Self
sedimentary, microscopic in the belly
of each erosive eon. Yes, Class, more eons.
Eon eon eon eon eon. Such is long staring.
Some say we are the universe
dreaming. But Cloud Boy must be
its nightmare. Because what else
could terrify a universe?
The Big Crunch? Falling? Being chased
by a bully universe? Trembling
at the junior-high blackboard
and gaping at the intolerable algebra?
Imagining names for every thing—some Adam
armed with ambition and a label gun?
Or maybe just Cloud Boy
seduced by the city's reflective glare, raped
by the tireless clamor of pop culture, O child

of star-dissolving technology, O non-starer.
As always, Class, you're bored.
All right, then sing 'Auld Lang Syne' with me.
The song reminds me of Scotland—
though I've never been to Scotland—
reminds me of my grandmother sailing
the gulf of her final years.
Sing it, god-dammit.
Extra credit for crooning.
Extra credit for knowing what crooning is,
my darling hip-hop dawgs and gangstas,
my dear bitches and hos, my precious
groupies of the insipid pop star, my sweet
little Emo babies lapping the whiny amnion
of MTV. I remember when it was born, that pop-
cultural Big Bang—years before
you were even a puff of hope
inside Mama's brain, a speck of amino acid
in Daddy's spine....
Hallelujah cubed, multiplied by amen.
Crap, *that* should have been your midterm.
My esteemed bizzles, If I had a dime
for every time pop culture acted sensibly,
I'd have a nickel.
Joel, your eyeballs are nickels: dull,
worthless. Melanie, your skull
is a cradle of ill-chosen words—
O flambiguous Melanie, O jankless jankey.
Lynette, while the planet's tectonic
plates are held together by your bubble gum,

they nevertheless grind toward catastrophe.
Sandeep, even your cells drool,
bored with the tiresome lecture
of your body.... Gang, I'm tired.
I've just arrived
from Luquillo, jewel of the Atlantic.
My DNA, still looped into hammocks,
stares off across tropical cytoplasm,
lagoons of primeval goo,
mitochondrial reefs, a dense nucleus
of sea-reflected stars....
Learn this well: my DNA shall not be
juggled with—it is, after all, an acid.
Ralph, I've dipped your prose
in acid: may your syntax improve,
may your adverbs bubble and dissolve.
Wendy, may you wander in late
to your own burial,
and may your closed casket gasp
open before swallowing you, Wendy.
Alex, Alex, Alex—plagiarist
of a memoir, may you discover the remote
little island of your own history,
O Conquistador of Failure, O Captain Sloth....
Class, I envy your infinite room
for change: 18 years old—what will happen?
At 18, I was your ancestor: same thumping
leg, same uninventive sarcasm
(my poor mother), same lack of verve,
same blind worship

of over-rated troubadours.
But at 32, the song remains the same.
Example: yawning mailbox.
Example: endless mugs of ale, smashed
alarm clocks. Smashed alarm clocks
litter my apartment: wherever I walk,
I kick through their broken skeletons—
Time's cracked ribcage, Time's splintered skull....
Can a person change at 32?
Can he get new molars, a new spine,
a new soul? I don't know
what a soul is. My father would be damned
to let his boys grow up
in a haunted house, to cower
in the cobwebbed attic of Religion.
Is the soul a haunted house?
Does it have paws, jaws, retractable claws?
Is it a machine, a black hole,
a hailstone? Does it glisten like nectar?
Is the soul a nebula of scattered atoms?
Is it a honeycomb, a sailboat, a willow, a ribbon
of neurons? Class, there's your god-
damned final exam. You'll earn one
of two grades: an A for showing
a proton of *self,* or an F for throwing
a wrench into the cosmic loom.
Nancy, don't worry—you've missed nothing
but the point. Emily, I lied—nobody cares
about the cuteness index of your fucking
puppy. Rebecca, may your trite suburb

be flattened by a cyclone
of cliché, and may you dangle
à la participle from the village gallows.
Stephanie, I wish you would drop
me a line next spring—you, the only one
for whom my little bells toll.
Antonio, may the hip nightclub you deem
a temple be evacuated during a scourge
of nauseating semi-colons. And Farley,
did you dream of a swarm of F's—thrumming
dragonflies envying your luminous inaction?
Class, I've tried to teach you
that you cannot toss envy into a corner
trashcan, that you cannot crumple
infinity like a hundredth essay draft.
More abstractions: absence, apathy,
arrogance—all lined up alphabetically,
the dictionary of your lives....
Alas, I cannot teach you how to learn
who you are, how to be perceptive.
Example: I'm certain that not one of you has paid
attention: do you really think
I'm writing to you from a vast continent
of ice and stone, a place where the stars
hang from cosmic hooks, and sway?
Ah, but I may as well be: the horizon
circles me, white and empty, a new page—
gloriously, gloriously blank.

Letter to Bonczek from Brockport

Michelle, Asia's underwater, and a wave
of rainy nostalgia descends
from the gray bowl of Lake Ontario,
where the feeble surf laps
at Hamlin Beach: mere cat spittle. *A butterfly flaps*
its wings in China, blah blah blah....
And on the coast of Thailand, along the scar
of the Maldives, geology and physics
have spoken: a lullaby about saltwater,
about broken huts, about toddlers
with lungs full of seaweed.
Who is he who needs further proof of God
as a fiction? Who is she who still climbs
the bell tower to sling prayers at the stars,
and who are they who cannot feel
the pinging hail of those prayers?
No stars here, Bonczek.
A black cloud 100 square miles thick
menaces this steepled village, arcs
into space: satellites get stuck
like moths in cotton. Panic
becomes terror when televisions fail to bark
the half-time babble, to rattle
the jewelry of the bachelorette, to herald
the swamping of a whole fucking continent.
Plasma screens idle, black and still
as the historic and mighty Erie Canal.
The dull canal oozes westward—
bargeless, waveless—toward the grim
stillness of Lake Erie.

I haven't seen sun, Michelle, since Luquillo—
where even the lines of latitude wail
sad *canciones,* and where the sun hangs
overhead even at midnight, the eye
of a compassionate god....
In other words: impossible.
I worry about vitamin D,
that I'll be rickets-stricken by Valentine's Day,
that my cells will swell with scurvy, burst
like little hearts. Hell, I'm not a pharmacist.
And praise Fortune I'm not a mailman!
All the local merchants have switched
places again—the book shop and diner,
the coffee shop and salon,
the head shop and saloon—
as though they revolve
round some soggy nucleus, impossible
to see—perhaps Nostalgia itself.
And I wonder if at the core of the Earth,
if at the center of the god-damned galaxy,
there spins such a bulky abstraction.
This rain is marvelously tangible,
as are the umbrellas swirling like black
pinwheels on these riverine streets.
Bonczek, many a moon has shriveled and swelled
since you split for Spokane, since I split
for Wherever with my beer belly,
my ragged knapsack, my tongue
lapping poems from the bowl of the world.
Everyone we knew has sprung

a litter, and pitchers of swill are a quarter
more, and our saloon—where we tossed
our bulls-eyes and swallowed our swill,
where we slung jeers
at lousy cover bands, where we drowned
and drowned in the basements
of innumerable pints, where we sunk
like closing-time eight-balls—
O our saloon is an attic
of televisions, and behind every black screen
a football spirals into its wide-open future,
a hockey puck sails
into a new and violent world....
But some things remain true.
Example: the crosswalk is still
a heap of mangled pedestrians struck
by local imbeciles, la la la.
Example: the continents still grind
their tectonic jaws, spilling panic and terror
into the salty throats of wretched islanders,
O treacherous geology, O cheerless physics....
And how about the elusive sun—
our stable G-class star which will never burn
this planet to supernova dust.
Dig it, Bonczek, we're alive
because of cosmic mediocrity!
Since last night, the saloon has moved again,
but let's find it—in the basement
of the post office, in the bell tower
of a church—and let's get impossibly drunk

on the slash of sun we know
must be up there. Michelle, let's toast it
as though it were indeed the watery eye of God:
Down the hatch, Sun, you fucking lemon—
how yellow and dull, how sour
in your absence.

Letter to Seaton from a Little Ice Age

Maureen, the city's a jungle
of icicles hanging like the fangs
of *Smilodon californicus* (so horrifyingly apt!)
from stop signs, oak branches,
tricycles, from icicles.... And titanic icicles
dangle from the Moon: our finest poets
shiver and swoon. That lousy café
where we slurped Pepsis and gaped
at tumorous calzones is a cave of ice.
The Frozen Foods aisle at Publix
is un-navigable, an icy tangle
of limp-wheeled carts and stunned housewives.
The deli reeks of Mastodon....
Pity us: holed up in heatless bungalows
stung by a chill as old and tired
as the Pleistocene. What new epoch
slouches like a continent of ice toward us?
Swingsets, martini glasses, bowls
of dog food—all museumed in ice.
Even the dependable postal service
is crippled—O how they once delivered
rejection slips heroically in sleet,
hail, tsunami, nuclear winter....
I'll bet five bucks (half my teacher's salary)
that even when the cosmos collapses
in a Big Crunch—when it crumples
like a failed poem—yes, even *then* these alleys
will teem with whistling mailmen
sifting through doomed postcards.
But this, Maureen, is too much. Mail

trucks have toppled, and their little wheels
spin dismal orbits. Disheveled mailmen
cartwheel over the ice. Postcards
from the tropics scatter like confetti.
The city's mailboxes are cocooned in ice.
The tavern next door is, somehow, open.
Can I get a *hallelujah?*
The cook's teeth chatter as he marvels
at idiocy—caravans of idiots slide sedans
across glaciated boulevards,
risk broken necks for a taco,
for a frozen pilsner: they chisel away,
suck on the shavings as they huddle
for warmth under neon signs.
A colossal tongue of ice laps Canadian plains,
laps across the Great Lakes—the lakes
stupefied by the irony—
down, down through Appalachia,
and on into 12th Street, Atlanta,
like another god-damned limousine.
My wall map itself is a cliché of ice,
and spiders skate spidery infinities
across state lines.
O I envy their mobility, and am heartened
by their will to enjoy themselves. So rare,
Maureen: a creature deliberately alive
when all other living things waste away
in a stink of unpleasantness, in their own
sour and contagious and miasmic muck.
Can I get an *amen?*

And what of the homeless, who slump
over trash-fires so feeble
the flames have frozen—the forked
fractals crumbling like kindling....
My brother overseas is convinced
it's 75 degrees here in 'Hot-lanta,'
that I must be wiping sweat with the sleeve
of my festive pineapple shirt as I watch ice
melt in a hammock-side margarita....
I would write him the truth,
but my mailman Wayne has been washed
away, poor fellow, by the waxing tide
of inaction: no mail on a Saturday.
Inconceivable.
Somebody ought to be handcuffed, shackled,
emaciated. I'll have to wait until Monday
to swim again in the surf
of rejection. Meantime, the city will suffer
an epic flood—all this ice melting
into a great river. If we had a town
crier, he'd scale our finest skyscraper
and cry, wailing in the new
age. Look at him, our crier, crumpling,
crumpling an obsolete map:
the very end—hallelujah, amen—
of the universe.

Letter to Riggs from Cobble Hill

Dearest Nina, I've just turned
33—'turned,' as though I'm a quart of milk
left too long in a college fridge.
I do feel chunky, out-of-date,
a little sour.... My birthday party
in Manhattan was flooded, and we all ended
up at Muldoon's on Third, sighing
into pints of Guinness, slipping crumpled
bills into the jukebox, pounding
the jukebox as taxis sailed uptown like arks.
Earlier, a double rainbow arced
an epic yawn over Brooklyn's Cobble Hill.
How romantic. 'Cobble Hill' sounds
like a neighborhood in San Francisco—
North Beach, say—some foggy nook peppered
with bistros now named after Kerouac
novels where Jack scribbled lousy haiku
on napkins, where Brautigan hung his gloominess
years before he scattered his graymatter
across a Marin bungalow....
Crap, maybe our betweeded mentors
were right: all poems flirt
with Death.
Think of all those bloody manuscripts,
the bullet-holed pages, the typewriters
bobbing in lakes of gin....
Nina, the caskets of the world
are crafted from recycled pencils!
Ashes fall like pencil shavings,
and we're erased. Humbug on Death,

that fogbound metropolis, that thunderclap.
Humbug on aging, that rising
sea level, that polar melt drowning the piers,
the pizza shops, the watering holes of Brooklyn.
And how did I spend my actual birthday?
Nine hours of non-stop PBR,
cackling at the silly horror
of junior high, at a dive called Floyd
(not Floyd's, mind you),
where in one afternoon you can roll
bocce balls on an alley of clay, guzzle
a 'crap-o-copia' of blue-collar American swill
(Schlitz, Nina!), and dig some live bluegrass—
nineteen hippies with banjos and steel-
strung spines: good times.
But even at 33, I've not grown up.
I still make asinine pinky bets
on the world's obscure minutiae, still strum
the strings of Last Call, still harbor
the juvenile dream of being
a real writer, like when I was 20
and discovered *On the Road:* O bible
of bibles, O clichéd influence, O ragged
jewel of the Albany Public Library.
Imagine, Nina: over the cytoplasmic pond
of each of my cells, a blue centerlight popped
and I went *Awww....*
For that I owe Kerouac's estate a nickel.
Crap—as ever, I'm growing
poorer, poor as I was at 20.

What a jackass I was—fired
from the mall ice cream shop,
living on saltines and sarcasm, all summer
planning the colossal
road trip I'd never take, tracing
a blue vein across America, O dusty map
of my failure, O hopeless artery.
And worse, typing abysmal fictions
about soulmates. Good god, why
didn't I burn them, heave the ashes
beyond the stratosphere where like meteorites
they'd ravage passing satellites?
Nina, I should have been a meteorologist,
spent my soaked birthdays calculating
wind-chill, typhoon velocity, frequency
of Asian monsoon. Stuck in Albany,
New York, winters I'd wail
the city's icicle-index, and the icicle-
index of my eyeballs, my spine,
my shrunken testicles.
I'd woo the gals at Sadie's with dew-
point babble, atmospheric something-or-others,
barometric what-nots, ozonic tomfoolery,
steamy gulf-stream hijinx, lusty
cirronimbus cumulostratus yammerings....
Meow!
One certainty: I'd compare hailstone size
only—O for love of the gods
to which I will not subscribe—yes,
only to softballs or golf balls lest I'd get fired

from the local affiliate for a molecule of originality.
Best of all, I would not be troubled
by metaphor,
nor obsessed with the tragic whore
of irony. Example: how gloriously blank
my face would have been when you told me
of that swampy night in swampy Greensboro—
your shirtless, muscled neighbor heaving
in the lamp-lit street, baying for his lost
hound: 'Stella! Stellaaaaa!'
But no, I love the alchemy:
how a sweaty frat boy invented irony
by accident, irony like gunpowder—
the cause of how much grief?
And don't forget our mentors,
who taught us that all writers must fall
in love with grief. . . .
Nina, great-great-great-great-etc.-great-
granddaughter of Emerson himself—
that miner, that digger, of grief—Nina,
descendant also of the first mucky pool
of protoplasm, you're my sister! How simple
our lives were then: no hangovers, no throbbing
telephones, no subway delays when we had to piss,
no broken shoelaces when there was no time,
no airplane missiles, and none of this
itchy, oppressive, throat-clenching humidity.
Brooklyn's a rainforest. Where is my machete
to hack through these bejungled streets?
O that I knew the science

of humidity! O that I lived in a Siberian igloo!
And O that I could retire
this archaic and melancholy-soaked *O*....
But Nina, my youth—I mean mouth—
is in perpetual howl
because despite my intolerable
lamenting, I adore this universe—
parallel to infinite and intolerable universes.
Out there, Nina, we're famous writers.
Our words echo like Big Bangs
in packed auditoriums. Still, I'll take this
lousy place—from the unreachable orbit of Pluto
to the Moon's lifeless chalk,
from the most far-flung quark
to Andromeda's dull halo,
from the theoretical lip of this cosmos
to the tangible lip of our atmosphere,
those scattered few glorious trace elements—
I fucking love the trace elements—
and all the way down
here to Cobble Hill: sundresses wagging
down Smith, amen, curbside nectarines, this sagging
humidity—even my skeleton is sweating....
I shall cross the harbor,
O Brooklyn Ferry, and wish a happy,
happy birthday to that clipped and wretched skyline
and all its marvelous crumple, and to mine.

Letter to Wright from Croton Point

James Wright, my god,
this ain't Goose Prairie.
Not that I've been to Goose Prairie,
but I can imagine the slap
of whitewater, the crawl of sage,
of milkweed—the western air speckled
with billions of wind-blown stars.
Any milkweed here has been trampled
under the bare, dirt-caked feet
of innumerable hippies. For a decade
I've volunteered at this folk festival,
the Great Hudson River Revival—
doing my microscopic part to save
this doomed planet, la la la,
and I've grown tired of the throngs
of hippies. I work in Peace
Keeping but I'm fixing to hurl
beer bottles, as my grandma would
have said, willy-nilly. Ah phooey,
I would very much like Godzilla
to emerge from the river, spit fire
across every disheveled goatee,
every greasy dread.
Hippies in the 21st century, James Wright—
this is like an Athenian Sophist convention
teeming with cavemen.
Ever the fool, I'd thought that after splitting
from my upstate college town, my life
would be hippie-free. That village is a hive
of hippies: my old ballcap still reeks

of patchouli and second-hand weed.
And curse whatever my soul is,
I even dated a hippie.
And now I'm surrounded by skirts
made from dishrags and rope, surrounded
by ragged acoustic guitars and hackeysacks
(sorry—'foot bags'), by devil sticks,
and by Doctor Seussian hats
that make the hippies' skulls appear
as if pulled into a black hole, some rift
in the paisley fabric of hippie space-time....
James Wright, such is contemporary
hippie nonsense.
Hippie hippie hippie hippie hippie.
Their tents rise like tepees
along the Hudson, *my* river—not as mighty
as your Ohio, and actually an estuary.
I was born 40
miles downstream. Like you I got the hell
out of my sloppy hometown,
which I can see from the edge of this
wooded parkland peninsula, seething.
I might have traded it for Martins Ferry—its mills
and riverbends, its factory spill,
its iron-bridge Americana.
When autumn begins in Yonkers, New York,
the hearts of coaches swell
and burst, and linebackers gallop terribly
against themselves....
Unlike you, James Wright, I grew up in a city.

Is the sorrow of a city more luminous
than the sorrow of a small town?
Is sorrow luminous?
To hell with abstract questions.
Instead: wind-chopped surf,
my hometown's water tower stabbing
the distant sky, one zillion dandelions, the dull
gray beams of the Tappan Zee.
I remember crossing it, imagining the whole
river in my little lungs, the surf sparking
my restless endoplasm, my infinite lament....
My granddad's Olds would dart
north, fishlike, into the glacial valley,
into summer's inflating balloon.
Look at the bridge now: a relic of my spent
childhood (O Auld Lang Syne), leaping
across my river—like I want to now,
assaulted by hordes of grizzled folksingers
yowling about garbage and the looming
tumors of nearby Indian Point.
Folksingers loathe nuclear power.
Shoeless, they compose silly songs,
scoot around in solar-powered Matchbox cars
pasted with über-left-wing bumper stickers
devoid of even a fucking quark of irony.
Example: I HATE REPUBLICANS!
Example: EATING ANIMAL MEAT IS WRONG!
Example: INDIAN POINT IS POLLUTING THE HUDSON,
THEREFORE YOU SHOULD WRITE A LETTER TO THE GOVERNOR
COMPLAINING TO HIM OR HER ABOUT THIS FACT!

Buggers, even I BRAKE FOR LIBERALS!
would have more wit.
Behold the exclamations!
This is because folksingers only holler.
Hollering is Lesson #1 in folksinger kindergarten,
where they do not build temples to the gods
of subtlety and nuance.
Even the willows here are ironic, weeping
polluted tears into the polluted river.
Crap, is that irony? I don't even know anymore.
But don't worry, the historic Sloop Clearwater
bobs on the waves, its sail
billowing like the flag of a glimmering utopia,
the blank map of an uncharted and pristine world.
And, amen, if the sloop isn't crammed
with folksingers! How heartening
when they pull cigarette butts and pop cans
from the river, strumming their hippie banjos.
I have never seen so many fucking banjos.
How brave these folk are, scooping radioactive mojo
whilst singing Pete Seeger songs.
37 folksingers, zero harmony: what gives?
Hell, Pete Seeger himself is out on the sloop!
He yowls a prehistoric yowl,
his stubble more ancient than Time's uncle,
certainly older than the radiant skeleton of Doctor J.
Robert Oppenheimer....
Tonight the Hudson glows,
and not from bioluminescent algae, or the Moon.
James Wright, tonight even the atoms

in my river are hippies: gathered in a circle
and wailing folksongs about half-lives,
about toxic tapwater, about a river
so clean you could see the bottom.
Look: the atoms are wrecking
their tiny throats, and I'm dying
and dying to break
into any kind of god-damned blossom.

Letter to Dockins from a Foreign Country

to converse about America and Eternity, a hopeless task
ALLEN GINSBERG, *Howl*

for BCD, born 19 July 2005, Paris

Benjamin, rookie explorer, welcome
to hurricane season. Again,
the Gulf coast awaits an alphabet
of tropical catastrophes, each a spiral
on a TV screen. Like you, Peanut,
when you sailed the sonogram
sea toward the open gulf
of this life, your DNA ribboned
like lemon twists along the rim
of an ancient impact crater.
Flood us, belly kicker. Tiny wind,
your daddy was born in the aftermath
of the Moon landing: a gaggle
of buzzcut patriots plunging through space,
plunging a windless dagger—I mean flag—
into lifeless lunar soil. Be suspicious
of such a heap of adjectives.
Seasoned wailer, may you wail
the wail of verbs: may you wiggle,
jive, and dazzle. May you flail,
kick, jump, and zaggle.
And may you continue to break
records, O tallest baby ever
born at Saint Vincent de Paul.
Do they have basketball stars in France?
Epic beanstalk, will you reach the Moon,

yank out that toy flag?
Will you rake those cartoon Moon-boot
scars? Don't get me wrong—thanks
to Capitalism and the one true
God, the Moon is American,
and, boy, do I love America!
Young Dockins, in these special times,
the President—I mean God—
forbid I suggest otherwise.
Hooray, the Moon is not Venezuelan!
Yippee, the planets are not Libyan!
Hwæt, the universe is not governed
by the Maldives!
America something-dollars and something-cents
August-something 2000-something.
I can't stand my own mind.
America America America America America....
I want to quit my thankless job
and recite my litany wearing nothing
but an American flag and an Eisenhower tattoo....
But here I slouch in America,
in this foreign country, anticipating
tempestuous Katrina—
her cradling arms, her lazy eye,
her big wet kiss.
The news-channel bobbleheads are bent
into the gale at 45-degree angles, soaked
like alley toms, hip-
deep in gulfwater, and curse
their idle decisions to swap shifts
with Carol or Steve, who are no doubt tits-up

in Nantucket, in Anchorage, sucking
on gin & tonics, limes swirling
like tiny citrus cataclysms....
Then again, meteorologists are the new
American rock stars, aren't they—
they need only emaciate themselves
on a diet of lint and aloofness,
skip the barber until next hurricane season
(next week), and learn three guitar chords,
and they'll be the fucking Ramones.
Ben, dig my fellow Americans—eyeballs
clinging like barnacles
to plasma screens—hoping
that the impending destruction will be name-brand:
Gap Misery, Tylenol Hopelessness, Evian Oblivion....
God—I mean the President—is certain
that this colossal storm cell is really a terrorist
cell, that the sky over New Orleans,
over Biloxi, will rain anthrax,
that droplets will sail and pop
like grenades over the bayou, that jets
of wind will smash our skyscrapers....
Missiles are always blooming on the prairie
of the President's brain. The smallest breeze
strums the alarms: a toddler sneezes
and local schools close, a kindergartener
blows out birthday candles and the terror
threat swells to Indigo, to Violet, to the color
of an empty universe.... Far-off
nephew, my country is not a country
of reasonable folks. At breakfast they sip

from glasses of gasoline, suck the pumps dry,
leaving them leaking and bewildered.
Look at my country-folk now, an Exodus
driving north, inland, to higher ground—
some Ararat of the American South.
In a few days, those left behind will have no choice
but to loot from rafts crafted from blown-off roofs.
They'll have to swim to church
through avenues of toxic swill,
and in full scuba gear ask their God
what-the-fuck, the submerged skyline a reef....
And as for the rest
of my countrymen, my fellow foreigners,
they'll send pennies through the mail,
and get right back to voting for their American
Idol, to scraping oil from the planetary core,
to perfecting the holy
art of Looking Fabulous....
Squealer, someday you'll be able to tell
me to shut up in a language I'll never learn,
save for the basics: *oui, merci, voilà,*
je ne parle pas Francais,
mon dieu, c'est terrible, bonne nuit Benjamin....
You'll grow up in a hurricane-
free zone, fling yourself through weatherless
weather on your bicycle, fan your birthday
candles with the harmless wind
of your breath—wishing for what?—
and play Superman at Halloween:
so many people to save.

Behold the Superdome, the s on its roof
more like a bulls-eye than a symbol
of hope or miracle.
It's crammed to its gills:
thousands peer from portholes
directly at Doom because here She comes
and She won't be stopped,
not even by the President's biggest tanks,
and New Orleans was built below sea level
by our earliest civic geniuses,
and She won't be stopped,
not even by my country's most ignorant
patriot, its longest missile,
not even by terrorists, and the word
of the day will be *water*—
or, as they say where you live, *l'eau*.
L'eau will be the word of the decade,
and a whole metropolis
will become an Atlantis, and what ever
will my country's co-eds do at Mardi Gras?
Vomit tequila laced with algae and silt?
Show their tits to alligators?
The Gulf of Mexico is a seething cauldron:
eye-of-newt, etc.
But you, littlest Dockins—
21st-century baby, metric baby, O triple
citizen of this planet—your crib is silent
and still. Ben, student of Zen, only a tiny fist
under your ribs closes and opens,
as though waving.

Letter to Iredell from the Yucatán

Jamie, once again I'm strumming the low
latitudes, plucking dark lines
like harp strings—oblivion's
tropical melody. All morning I've been drinking
the wide blue sky: cliché heaped upon cliché—
each atom complicit, each molecule a temple
of triteness, a dull world.
But this green sea is a global original,
an inimitable canvas. And beyond the epic
reef that stretches like a marine spine
toward Belize: the zillion
hotels of Cozumel—a zillion fangs
in the jaw of the horizon, the horizon
speckled with cruise ships fatter
and no doubt more festive than my hometown.
Hometown, I have failed
to miss you....
I'm surrounded by emaciated Europeans,
by the entire citizenry of prairie Canada,
and by innumerable slobs
thrashed by the American Rust Belt,
where the song of polluted snow
whines non-stop on every snowbound stereo,
the slushy dirge of the merciless Great Lakes—
souvenirs from a mythic Ice Age....
Manhattan, too, is somewhere
under 26 inches of blizzard—as alien
to these latitudes as an alarm clock,
as commuter gridlock, as sagging hopes....
Jamie, I hereby make the same threat

I made last winter in Luquillo:
I shall not return—to where I'm mired
in Theory, where my students think
I'm a joke, where I pass lagoons
of time slumped over poker tables, where I lust
after an endangered species:
sleep. *Eventus raritus.* What am I
hoping to escape? Apocalypse? No luck.
Why, just today I jammed my apocalyptic big toe
against an apocalyptic beach rock.
Metatarsal apocalypse!
Maybe this apocalyptic wound will keep me
here—O throbbing, apocalyptic serendipity.
American Customs is certain to reject
my foreign injury, my apocalyptic lament....
Luckily, Jesús at the beach bar has plenty of ice,
and *cerveza. Cuatro,* please, Jesús—O holy
amigo. No, fuck it, *ocho.*
Look, Jamie, with a sprained toe
it's difficult to distill the world into plastic
cups of metaphor, pints of imagery.
I'm engulfed by images—all that potential.
But so is every dumb-ass on this planet. Sadly,
99.9% are oblivious, their senses
dulled by cinematic tomfoolery, dulled
by feeble television plots, dulled
by the predictable Hollywood antics
of husky blue-collar suburban dads.
Dulled, Jamie, by fake tacos.
Nevertheless, the rest of us could populate

a small city, a great city....
Describing the tropics is a recipe
for cliché. Still, amen to the gaggles
of rookie parasailers, the marvelous constellation
of thatch cabanas—such galactic simplicity.
Amen to the coconut trees, their joblessness.
Amen to the diving pelicans and gulls—
I wish I spoke Pelican, fluent Gull.
I wish I could make a living
being amazed. And triple amen to the swagger
of Mesoamerican thighs....
I have not forgotten my big toe.
Each thump of my pulse is another beach rock.
And since misery is a magnet
for misery, my wisdom tooth—à la
wisdom toe—is impacted, la la la.
Wisdom, my ass—unless wisdom
is really a species of pain,
which I suppose it has always been.
Jamie, it comes to this: *I cannot explain*
my suffering—the nucleus of all
literature, all life. Suffering itself is tolerable!
But don't we desire somebody
to know it? And isn't this futile?
I may as well wear the horizon
around my neck, may as well snap
the sun like a yo-yo, may as well turn
my cytoplasm to saltwater.
I may as well expect Immortality
to arrive like a tax refund—

my poor mailbox suffering
an ancient and colossal envy....
Crap, I'm a contemporary Gilgamesh.
I swear on Enkidu's maggoty corpse
that if I see the sail of Utnapishtim's
pre-Old-Testament ark
rippling lovely Sumerian ripples
toward this post-New-Testament beach,
I'll leap aboard and forever lap tequila
with the planet's trillion-and-a-half species, amen.
And speaking of the Impossible, I've met a gal
from Vancouver—let's call her
Toodles. I'm not spicy enough for Toodles,
not Latino enough, not muscular enough,
not jar-headed enough. Et fucking cetera.
I'm the little engine that couldn't,
that can't, that doesn't, that hasn't,
that won't, that might've been, that isn't,
that will never be. O my soul
is, and always will be, a factory
of verb tenses, a mill of uselessness.
Toodles is lovely while I'm broken and lame
and crippled and torn and busted and dim
and wounded and sad and fractured and grim
and crooked and chipped and jaded and dumb
and mopey and old and pasty and damned
and hollow and bent. Curses, now I'm a god-
damned adjective factory.
I'm white as the Moon, and chunkier—
O decade of ironic excess, O graduate school....

If consciousness is the universe
thinking, then Toodles is a light bulb,
a spark of genius, a luminous
and pulsing neuron, the discovery
of a rare, an impossible, metal.... No matter.
Tonight I will swim a reef
of tequila bottles, flirt with married gals,
swallow a disastrous *habanero,*
and wake tomorrow with all the conquistadorean
swords slashing my skull to atomic debris,
stirring my guts to an angry, bubbling muck....
Welcome to my vacation!—busted
toe, throbbing jaw, agave hangover,
pepper revenge, and the 697th sweetie
I'll never have. A sense of failure
is all I have. I'm a fat, griping *gringo.*
Nevertheless, nothing shall be ruinous
to my week off from the States:
not Dutch Boy kicking my ass
at nine-ball, not my sunburned armpits,
my sunburned bald spot,
not the black hole seething
at the back of my jaw, dense and perilous,
not Toodles growing more lovely
with each nanosecond (and exponentially
more aloof—she's swelling into a fucking parabola
of aloofness), not even the menacing squall
that this evening will appear as a wall
at the horizon, as a dark skull
over Cozumel—its empty eye sockets

trained on the Riviera Maya.
So. *Ocho mas cervezas,* O saints
many-fisted in Oblivion, O free beer.
Because you know what, Jamie?
I have conquered Mexico: I've scaled *Nohoch Mul*
(translation: 'large hill'—fucking hyperbole-
starved Mayans!), a pyramid 42 meters
above the Yucatán jungle, microcosm
of the entire biosphere.
Look, if I'm Señor Sucker, and the Earth
really was baked in a cosmic oven
by some vowel-less beast, by ________,
then this is surely what the inventive genius
had in mind—jungled canopy yawning
seaward for mile upon canopied mile.
You can see the fucking Azores,
and that's just not good for the eyes.
Ditto the nineteen trillion
tour-bus imbeciles in Steelers jerseys
and flip-flops—the planet's intolerable
and inescapable protoplasm....
Climbing down was unparalleled
vertigo terror—not of falling but of landing,
O inflexible planet.
But god-dammit all to hell, Jamie,
I did not geek out and pray to the void—
and it is a void out there, or *in* there, or wherever
is that space of sublime mystery, of the numinous,
something I'm always trying to gather.
I wish I could gather Toodles,

who just sailed by with a maddening little wave
and with a smile that I want
to both kiss and punch—O Impossibility.
And it's impossible, though true,
that soon I'll grumble in the belly of a jet,
then slouch in a taxi to Midtown, then swivel
on a stool at Vickery's where we'll throw back
some Don Julio (imported—sad sad sad),
extra limes, babble
our usual two-bit barroom babble,
and toast to inflexible reality....
From the plane I'll watch the Yucatán
peninsula bend west, then south, and I'll recall
that in the beginning was The Word,
and I'll mumble that Word—a vowel-less
monstrosity that doesn't quite know
what it has just created, and as Mexico
drifts behind me, maybe forever,
I'll mutter that Word over and over,
my sad little mantra:
Toodles, Toodles, Toodles, Toodles, Toodles....
You see, Jamie, even at the very beginning
was the essence, the germ,
of goodbye.

Channeling Dockins, Iredell Replies from Breadloaf

Two-bit Dockins, you goon, what the fuck
is the capital of Uzbekistan? Not capital
like capital city—like exotic metropolis
teeming with rickshaws and zeppelins
and ziggurats—but capital like capital*ism*,
like what do the merry Uzbeks use to buy
salt and trinkets? O I've been struggling
with a poem about Marx, and it's evolving
into swill with each bourgeois penstroke,
each sip of Jameson. Ha, you expected me
to name a vodka, to maintain the integrity
of the motif, but vodka is fucking dumb.
The grizzled cabbie in grizzled Burlington
let me pitstop for whiskey and for smokes
I don't need (don't rat me out to my old lady),
and he didn't even charge me for the idling.
O Buggers Curses Crap, I felt like a god-
damned dirty hippie. You like that one,
Enjambment Boy? And could such a miracle
ever visit poor taxi-less Uzbekistan? Hell,
do its villages still suffer the interminable
bread lines? Do rusted Soviet tanks still
wait to fire cheerless Communist shells
through the icy hula-hoop of the Arctic Circle
and into the brains of fat Kansans, of Panhandle
prom queens, of 300,000,000,etc.-illion
brainless Americans? How close is Chernobyl,
its humming sidewalks, its conifer needles
tapping tapping tapping to the plutonial
metronome of half-lives? Are American

cigarettes, American blue jeans—O endless
contraband spilling like uranium marbles
from the endless American toybox—still all
the rage two decades after that first totalitarian
brick was untotalitarianly unloosed? Curses,
I tire of questions. The Vermont stars spell
a marvelous answer—each a luminous
fragment of a scattered Unified Field Theory.
They launch photons through the Arctic
air of these August evenings, and alongside
each photon, a teenaged Albert Einstein pops
a wheelie on a quantum 19th-century bicycle....
You like this cosmic *mise en scène,* Cosmology
Boy, Admiral Quark? You and your god-damned
science ought to be caged in a mitochondrial
prison, a heartless gulag in some solar Siberia....
Ahem. Meantime, it's *literally* 4,000 degrees
in Atlanta—isn't it, Über-Hyperbole Boy?—
and you've been dragging your Sisyphusian
knapsack down muggy Peachtree, sweltering
10th, insufferable Charles Allen.... Thanks
for feeding my two-bit cat. How is that little
gangster? Has his needy mewing distracted you
from your epic rants, your Odyssean tirades,
your idiotic—I mean Iliadic—invectives?
Last I heard from you, you were complaining—
to the full astonishment of Western civilization.
No, fuck it—Eastern civilization, too. Throngs
of water-logged Indonesians, of soaked Sri Lankans,
of Thai, of Madagascarians, of doomed Maldivians,

have gathered on tsunami-wrecked beaches
to gasp a simultaneous global gasp whenever
Dockins complains. You like that, Sarcasm
Boy? I'll fucking bury you in irony, Irony Boy.
But not before you finish cat-sitting Jules,
who must also be sweating, who must also
think that the August sun is a lousy goon.
I've seen Jules pant. A panting kitty-cat
is an odd thing: I expect it to fetch the useless,
useless newspaper, to bark at the mailman,
his infinite heap of sour news.... Good news
here—an uninterrupted party: night after night
of glorious campfire, of glorious stars streaming
down their total and glorious lack of capital—
i.e. *pesos,* or whatever the fuck the merry Uzbeks
use to capture the American illusion. Meantime,
the starlight whips the campfire into dizzying
fractals. You like that one, Geometry Boy?
I haven't forgotten my Marx poem, failing
like a doomed *ism*. Nights I slouch—your pet
word, eh, Comet Boy?—nights I slouch fireside,
telling riotous stories of my riotous West Coast
youth, my riotous, untamed *bildungsroman.*
You like that word, Dockins? I'll pass
my exams for sure, and two-bit goons across
the globe will have to call me 'Doctor.'
But no one here has been very productive.
Example: this one homeboy Steve is failing
to compose a villanelle about pelicans.
What jackjob writes poems about pelicans?

Essays, even. Novellas, pamphlets, graffiti,
and all manner of two-bit literary what-not.
My roommate Rupert can't even bang out
a decent double sestina over juice and waffles.
And what's with all these Formalists, anyhow?
You'd grumble so loud—your throat a calamity
of scotch, your irises sad little tectonic
mills—that the planet would tilt hopelessly
on its feeble axis, crack like a sourball....
But then there's Melanie. Mike, you'd adore
Melanie—she hasn't written a single word.
Daily she waits for the Earth to darken, to bend
toward the stars so she can exhort them.
You like that word, Word Boy? O Melanie,
Melanie, who exhorts the stars to burst.
We can almost hear the stars asking her
politely—we imagine the stars are polite—
to shut the fuck up, poor poemless Melanie.
Poor poemless All of Us, trapped between
flames. Flames up there, flames down here—
it's fucking transcendental, *très* Thoreauvian.
I shall keep a fifteenth eye open for Thoreau
to amble over yonder hill—one of Vermont's
trillion quaint little god-damned yonder hills—
his beard twinkling with starlight, with ink,
with pond ice, with crumbs of the two-bit Void,
a yawping Walt Whitman swinging à la Tarzan
through his viney beard.... Seems to me a poem
about Marx is a retarded idea, though I'm blind
to the capital of Uzbekistan—I mean the city

this time. I bet you would know, Geography Boy,
you walking atlas, atlas with kidneys, lungs,
Golgi apparati, fucking gills—the impossible
weight of infinite place-names bee-stinging
your shoulders. Oh exponential hell! A pox
on this blessed plot—this erupting volcano,
this Belizean haiku, this monsoon, this England—
of mixed metaphor. Dammit, I'm global, too:
patron saint of Monterey, Sal Paradise of Reno,
Huckleberry Finn of the northing Salinas,
notorious bunny-killer of the Basin and Range,
and unchallenged master of Mexican-gang
Spanish—the only lexicon I use with Jules,
so if he's been ignoring you, Mike—sorry.
Try *pinche puta*. I'll translate at Vickery's
over a pint, our 100,000th—limes for you,
intolerable Scurvy Boy, and I'll go limeless—
and we'll throw them down until the stars
ask us to please stop, until both of us, slouching
a terrific slouch, tilt our swooning heads away
from the splintered continents, push our palms
as if in prayer into the sad, sad humidity, aim
our burning throats starward and say—politely,
as though crooning—'Bitch, call me Doctor.'

Letter to Li Po from Vickery's

Home. I knew it entering.
RICHARD HUGO

Li Po, everything comes down
to this: I've got nothing genuine
left to say as football season drags
its intolerable ice age across the dark continent
of my patience. Stadiums seethe
with shirtless bullies scuba diving
inside helmets of stale swill,
scraping knuckles and skulls on reefs
of predictable American aggression.
The suburbs are a deathscape
of chicken wings and plasma screens.
Footballs whiz like bullets
across cookie-cutter cul-de-sacs.
The god of corn chips is a happy, happy god:
fatter than a Buddha, fatter than a universe,
its fat grin a sloppy constellation.
The suburbs are a kindergarten of high-fives,
a hive of ignorance. Example: the suburbs
have never heard of The Banished Immortal,
nor have they stared into the abyss
of Lu Mountain Waterfall.
Rebuttal from the suburbs:
Is that some kinda football team?
Take me to school, O Suburbs,
for my palms are not callused and raw
from that deafening circus of high-fives....
News since your death: the subway,

the submarine, the rotten, rotten suburbs.
I'm scribbling these letters thirteen centuries
after you scribbled poems into the luminous
dirt of Lu Mountain. Eccentric recluse,
I think we would have been pals—8th-century
China, 21st-century postmodern metropolis,
or somewhere amidst the timeless
Star River, upon which, even tonight,
the sail of your legend swells
big-bellied in cosmic wind, amen.
Only a genius would leap
into a river to embrace the Moon,
but only an idiot would survive.
You are a genius. Meantime, I've taken
the Idiot's—I mean Poet's—vow
of poverty, and my favorite spot in town
is a tavern: rivers of booze, infinite
rivers rivering down from the majestic Star....
Who says Vickery's, too, couldn't be a crossroads
of genius, like the bucolic wine shop
near Lo-yang where, circa 744, you stumbled
into the obsequious and tease-able
Tu Fu, Tu Fu emaciated
from all those poems he'd been suffering over.
I hope that 34th-century diggers—
with their unfathomable tools, in whatever
unfathomable dystopia may darken
this hallowed corner of the planet—
unearth my lost poem,
'Teasing Li Po,' translated from god-

knows-what Chinese ideograms,
which I'll someday scrawl into the luminous
dirt of this patio garden as bums sail up Crescent
on sad rafts of hopelessness....
Here goes: *For decades Li Po and the illustrious*
Mike Dockins tore it up at Vickery's—
even on school nights.
A crappy poem, but Hell Yeah.
You'd like this place: plenty of wine, plenty
of whining. Example: the jackasses on the satellite
radio are screeching about a gal named Lump.
She's Lump, Li Po. She's Lump, she's Lump,
and now she's in my head—a fucking tumor.
News since your death: the ragged
San Francisco Beats, the Beatles, *Teen Beat*.
News since your death: the American Revolution,
the French Revolution, the Industrial Revolution,
Lenin's revolution, Lennon's 'Revolution,'
1,244 more Earth revolutions
around its industrious star....
Meantime, I'm screeching my revolutionary lust
to a cold Pabst and a kicker of quality
tequila, rocks, because a cute girl I like
to call 'Worthless' is blowing smoke at me,
each lung a nebula, each lip a ruptured star.
You'd dig Worthless: the drunk
art major—flirty and aloof, a paradox
in cleavage and mascara, and supernova lips
whence all of the planet's comic and tragic matter....
News since your death: the atom

bomb, the carpet bomb, the Irish Car Bomb.
News since your death: the jet engine,
the kamikaze pilot, the Kamikaze.
News since your death: the Spanish
Civil War, the Crimean War,
the tireless raids of the tireless Mongols,
the War to End All Wars and its ironic
sting, the fucking Crusades.
News since your death: FEMA, Zima,
terza rima, an American flag on Iwo Jima,
Pizarro's blood seeping from the church bells of Lima.
News since your death: sonar, radar, gay-dar.
News since your death: the seismograph,
the photograph, the phonograph, the polygraph,
the mimeograph, the telegraph, the telegram,
the hologram, the mammogram, the numinous
pulse of the sonogram.
News since your death: FedEx, Tex-Mex,
hypertext, phone sex, the suburban
cinema multiplex, the museumed ankle,
metatarsal, spine, and fang of T-Rex.
News since your death: Silicon Valley,
silly string, string theory.
News since your death: antivenin, antibiotics,
Auntie Em, Auntie Em!
News since your death: I-95, the iPod,
live video stream of volcanoes
blossoming from the asthenosphere of Io,
O scandalous eye of Galileo,
E-I-E-I-O....

Sorry. Got carried away. But you know, Li Po, *how*
in the smoky recess of bars all over the world, a man
will suddenly dance because music, a juke box, a Greek
taverna band, moves him and how when he dances we
applaud and cry go. Cry *go* for me.
I don't want to die, but I can rattle off
a forest of Hudson Valley ponds—Arthur's, Tamarack,
Upper, Sphagnum, Bog Meadow, Aleck
Meadow—into which I would dive
the eternal dive if I could swallow the Moon
with its full tank of terrible water and die
a genius, celebrated by 34th-century poets
in their unfathomable province,
with their unfathomable hyperbole.
This would beat heart failure—
O dull and prosaic American fate....
News since your death: singed maps
of the Americas, satellite maps of China,
its Great Wall, a digital map of chromosomes.
Li Po, the human genome has been conceived,
sketched, sculpted, and mugged.
The human genome has been effectively mined.
And no bearded, scurvy-stricken Spaniard—
suffering ill-tempered natives, ill-tempered
fleas, and mutinous, rum-soaked deckhands—
had to circumnavigate the planet
to achieve it. The brain of Science exploded:
its graymatter has splattered across every jungle
and desert, every steppe and tundra,
every timber forest and prairie sprawl....

As I've said to the luminous sweetie-pie Allison Jenks
(who is, thankfully, also news since your death),
I'm not done.
Every cape and caldera, every alp
and canyon, every Mesozoic fossil bed,
every sand dune and palisade, every crumb
of lithosphere, every esker and drumlin,
cirque and arête, every woodland reservoir,
every gulf, every reef, every fjord
and tectonic plate, iceberg and geyser,
moraine and alluvial fan, every atoll
and peat bog, every microscopic archipelago,
every fucking icicle, and every thing of all
the 10,000 Things cluttering this doomed planet—
nowhere is it possible to escape the avalanche
of Science. What am I saying? Hallelujah!
I shall drink to this in Oblivion, pal of pals.
Yet despite the innumerable
acrobatic vaultings of Science,
our significance in the cosmos remains just
as feeble, our understanding of it weer
than the weest wee thing, that thing
for which even a lepton is staggering.
And how to explain the lepton, the blogosphere?
How explain the dog Laika, the chimpanzee
Koko, the sheep Dolly? How explain napalm,
Nagasaki, the incendiary synapses
firing missiles across Albert Einstein's brain?
How explain Google Earth, or the radiant
Nevada mountain named after the harmless

yucca—O grim tomb
where our most treacherous particles
will forever celebrate their tiny atomic birthdays....
Human hubris has ballooned: it now makes infinity
look like a nucleus of carbon. Example:
motorized buggies probe the colons
of dyspeptic septuagenarians.
Example: motorized buggies probe Pacific
trenches, the trenches of Mars. *Mars,*
Li Po. The Wanderer itself—
zigzagging retrograde across the fixed stars.
As I compose a letter to you, terrestrial Wanderer,
from Ye Olde Watering Hole—as my carbon
decomposes by clockwork half-lives, as neutrinos
soar and spiral like irksome footballs
through the dismal suburbs of my endoplasm,
as a seven-legged spider in this barroom corner
dies its unfathomable spidery death, as universes
and quarks by the nanosecond pop
like flash bulbs in and out of existence, as a physicist
moons over his little theory of strings, as a drunk
poet drowns in a moonlit river,
as the weedy American suburbs
creep their interminable weedy creep,
as my neighbors tremble and bend
before the capricious gods of Coin Flip,
Touchdown, and Sack,
and, amen, as the lovely Worthless blows me
one of her maddening smooches—yes,
even now that planet-jumping buggy is dragging

its little motor and its little American flag
(made in Taiwan) and its little infrared lenses
and its little wheels and its little gears
and its little cameras through the vast,
rusty canyons of Mars, clicking postcards of god-
knows-what wretched topography,
what cheerless terrain,
so that fat tourists on overcrowded buses
can have their thrilling visions of the cosmos....
Well, hell.
I need a fucking vacation. I'm also fishing
for a new name, something reclusive and mysterious:
Sagittarius, Boötes, Po.
O Li Po, Li Po, what is your first name?
Let me execute that question
as would those silly Oulipo cats
(more horrifying aptness!)
in their silly salons with their silly berets,
with their silly scissors and silly entropy:
is what name your first? name your first what is?
your what is name first? first what is your name?
is your first name what? Marvelous!
O I am an American of the most sublime order
of ignorance. Curses, I'm worse than the suburbs....
News since your death: a whiz kid
from Wapakoneta, Ohio,
while the planet watched, waddled
upon the Moon, stabbed it with a flagpole.
This is what America does best: stabbing,
slashing the cosmos, and like Zorro

leaving it in tatters, O bleeding cosmos....
Rebuttal from the cosmos: *No pity.* So.
Cheers, Friend. 'A little wine returns me
to the moon,' you wrote, and it did.
This is still happening: time does not exist.
Like me, you are alive and you are still
dying. The Moon, disguised as moonlight,
has leaped into a sliver of the great Star—
some Yangtze backwater.
Fool Poet, Genius Wanderer,
you leap in after it: to embrace, to mine,
to drink.

Letter to Meserve from Orgeval

Hallelujah, Susie, I'm finally developing
a taste for fine scotch—the zing
of peat in the throat, the spark
and snap of ice, the lovely radiance
in my skull. I have no idea
what's more impossible than a winter
holiday spent sober. A wheezing proton?
A planet shaped like a ukulele?
My French improving? *Mon dieu,* I've been lost
in Orgeval, practicing my feeble grammar
with tolerant Orgevalians: *je suis blah*
blah blah. . . . I'm disturbed
that even the local spiders are more fluent—
their webs a-tremble with spider-sized copies
of Proust, Flaubert, the translated
Lolita—taunting me
from tiny spidery throats.
I've been reduced to wretched
recipes—charades and American gibberish:
a sprinkle of *ers,* a dash of *ums.*
I ask for a scotch and get thrown out.
I ask to get thrown out and get a smooch.
I ask for a smooch and get a scotch.
Appalling. To master French I'd need five
tongues, 317 more lip muscles.
This is an apt occasion for a 'moreover.'
Example: Moreover, even my toddler nephew
can out-French me. This is the same kid who
staggers at his own Achoo,
clomps piano keys with his choo-choo,

wails at the tiniest boo-boo.
When Big Ben coos his nonsense coo,
murmurs his goobledygoo, his goo-goo-
ga-joob, I know he's calling me a buffoon,
a rascal, a scallywag, a two-bit goon,
a porky American. *Ich, ich, ich, ich....*
Ho Ho Ho, to the natives I must look
like Santa Claus, waddling
down the Rue de Gauthier hill delivering
my icicled beard and my icicled beer belly
to the *brasserie* where I have space
and peace because the non-smoking room
is populated only by me and my scribbles.
The front room is an oxygenless nebula.
Still, by sundown my lungs
will be tumorous balloons....
But what matters, epic traveler, is change
of latitude, to spring à la cricket
across this planet, even to creep
toward the Arctic Circle, which cannot be
far from this hamlet. The razor
wind shaves my stubble, and the sky
is a celebration of continuous darkness:
I keep expecting the Borealis
to splash its swirlies (swirl its splashies?)
on the horizon—openest of all open books....
Who's winning the hockey game
between the polar bears and timber wolves?
Where are the swarms of walrus
and reindeer, the ice-fishing Lapps?

Where are the barking seals, the emaciated
captives barking sorrow from frozen gulags?
Where are the orcas leaping the harbor
floes, and where is the harbor?
Where is the Inuit hootenanny,
the little street of igloos?
Susie, Polaris hangs inches above the chimneys
of Orgeval—glitters like a Christmas tree ball,
sways like a lantern—but offers no heat.
Alley cats swat its dazzling, dangling yarn....
Atlanta, by contrast, is the core
of the sun—nine hours away by postmodern
jet, half a day's work according to the gospel
of the American Work Ethic.
And I worked to get here: an autistic
toddler in 32D kicked
my seat for nine fucking hours. Sick, sick, sick, sick.
My circles of Hell crumpled into dismal trapezoids,
my vertebrae fossilized with metatarsals....
The girl's parents offered nothing
but sympathetic shrugs. And mercy
was nowhere when we landed
in freezing rain and darkness (8:31 AM)
at an airport shaped like the germ
of the Apocalypse.
But we're nigh on the birthday
of the little baby Jesus away in a manger
on a silent night O holy night round yon virgin
O come ye O come ye to Bethlehem,
so I was heartened to see the bereted,

be-rifled, be-khaki-ed militia
pacing Charles de Gaulle, waiting
for an oblivious tourist (is there a French equivalent
of *gringo?*) to take his eye for a nanosecond
off his knapsack so they could ravage it
with righteous, God-shaped bullets.
A *bientôt,* mini-pretzels! *Au revoir,* toothbrush!
Adieu, crossword puzzle!
We just don't see this kind of thing stateside,
do we?—this would gall and terrify
the insufferable yokels of Twin Forks,
of Council Springs, of Grand Bluffs,
of MiddleTown, U.S. of god-damned blessed A.
American airports seethe with evildoers—
or so Fearless Leader has avowed.
Decider of All Things,
He hurls down His oily Olympic Decisions:
evildoers hiding in passports, in Happy Meals,
between the oily teeth of escalators....
Here, evildoers hide only in thermometers:
the continental mercury has plummeted—
O treacherously warming globe—beyond all hope
of a reasonable cosmos,
O damp, drizzly December in my soul....
And at the bus stops of Orgeval, at Yuletide,
you can catch passing icebergs
into town, or over to ex-pat Poissy,
and this stuns no one.
The townsfolk, from their bucolic
doorsteps, wave to the iceberg driver,

who waves back, and despite the discomfort
it's all very charming. Orgeval
has no lack of rustic steeple or steep
cobbled hill, no lack of horse and donkey pasture.
Ben likes to visit the donkeys,
and when he says *donkey* in French,
I know that he's calling me one, that lovable imp.
And in the countryside, a peppering of chateaus.
Remember *Bon Voyage, Charlie Brown*—
when the chateau almost burns down?
I raise my glass to Snoopy.
Before he arrives with Woodstock
to insouciantly hose the flames, he skulks
in a cellar pub, amen, all dolled up
as the Flying Ace (scarf, goggles).
He rolls nickels into the jukebox, bays
to 1940s pop standards,
growing sentimental and drunk, sulking
over frosty root beers. But all he needs
is a sip of a new root beer to stifle whatever
sorrow a beagle suffers.
'Moonlight Serenade' drops
and there he goes with his wail and yelp....
Pastoral scenes must bore you, Snoozie—
you who have unearthed Antarctic pyramids,
chiseled ice off the windshields of a zillion
entombed spaceships,
sculpted a replica of Machu Picchu
from your mitochondrial marble,
discovered the East

Pole, questioned the holy creator
of plate tectonics.... Thanks for the weather-
stained postcards—21st-century Columbus,
poet Magellan, postmodern Byrd....
I'm adding Meserve to my list of famous explorers.
Your postcards sing of *cerveza,* of *cerveja,*
of however they say 'beer' in the Maldives,
if they even have beer in the Maldives—
poor Maldives! In any case, I love that song.
I sing it almost every day.
Susie, your postcards are the lusty
neon of distant cities—cities that have been bombed—
cities whose names have too many consonants,
or too few. Your postcards
are the magma that alters this planet,
the atlases of Elsewhere.
Sometimes, back home, stuck in the miraculous
dullness of Composition & Rhetoric,
and no way out except to be thankful
I'm not homeless—O impossible rent-free life,
I grade papers for a fucking roof—
sometimes I wish I could Tarzan-swing
the vines of longitude, the ropes of latitude,
to iceless Kilimanjarian slopes, to the Gobi
speckled with the skulls of Triceratops,
to the piranha-frenzied Amazon, to Lisbon's
starry, starry harbor, to the farthest
and tiniest and most tsunami-wrecked Aleutian,
to wherever
you've been. Hell, I'll even dive

your postcard pools, raft
your postcard rapids, scale your postcard alps.
Your knapsack is torn beyond repair
but well-loved, O velveteen knapsack.
Your eyeballs are little worlds,
an incalculable circumference.
And your passport, Odyssean
globetrotter, is a great library full of terror
and awe, and I hope it doesn't burn
at the whim of ignorant goons, O wretched,
wretched history of the world....
The land of Gilgamesh is still aflame,
and far beyond the heroics of any clever beagle.
For 50 centuries, even the sand has been nurturing
vicious *isms*. Someday, little sand airplanes
will swerve in terrible directions....
Ah hell, it's Christmas!
What I want, I'll never get: a box
of sand, so I could spend fireside evenings
counting the grains of human misery,
and marvel at the impossible number....
And where in the world
is Susie Meserve? Wherever
you are, *Joyeux Noël*.
I haven't seen you since we lifted mugs
to your fancy papers, to your leaping
free of graduate school, O lucky
magnificent bastard, too many Decembers ago.
I really do miss you most of all, Scarecrow—
our treks into piney Massachusetts hinterland,

those vacations from the hopeless
freshman essays piled like ironic gifts
on our hopeless desks,
our mornings with the eccentric and brilliant
and be-scarved Slovenian poet
(I still cannot effectively enunciate *Ljubljana*),
our bus rides across the Route 9 bridge
to Northampton—Thoreau's serpentine Connecticut
wrinkled with moonlight, swollen with lunar mojo....
Send me a postcard, Susie—from San Francisco
or the Andes, from Oregon or the Orinoco,
from north of Boston or a Bolivian prison,
from Deception Island or Monster Island—
I need news from Susieville.
The news from Mikeyville is grim: I've been sleeping
in the basement, and my spiderometer is,
as my pal Tony Moon would say,
off the chain. It's been wagging
like the tail of an anxious beagle—
four and counting. If I see a fifth,
I'm finding a hotel. Crap, with my French
I'd end up in the Pyrenees, in the Mariana Trench,
in a dark Martian trench, wandering
the Kuiper Belt in search of a pay phone,
desperately lost in downtown
Oort Cloud, O infinite
hyperbole.... I've named each spider
'Gregor Samsa'—O monstrous vermin.
Poor Gregor—maybe I too would have flung
the devastating apple....

Thus my Plea to the Spider World:
go menace some other universe.
And that's where hyperbole fails,
where it dims like an exhausted star:
a basement spider lurking even at the distant lip
of this universe—spinning threads
around quasars from its little spidery loom—
is too close. The ones in my room are nothing
like French poodles, i.e. dainty, i.e. elegant.
I am so fucking tired
of adjectives. In reverse
alphabetical order, these fuckers are:
wicked, vulgar, vituperative, violent, vile, vicious,
venomous, upsetting, unspeakable, unseemly,
unpleasant, unfair, underhanded, uncouth,
unacceptable, ugly, treacherous, terrible,
tasteless, tactless, suspicious, startling, spiteful,
spineless, sketchy, sinister, sinful, sickening,
shifty, scandalous, ribald, revolting, repulsive,
repugnant, reprehensible, repellent, profane,
precarious, pitiless, perilous, ominous, offensive,
odious, obscene, obnoxious, noxious, nefarious,
nauseating, nasty, monstrous, merciless,
malicious, malevolent, low, loathsome, jarring,
irregular, intolerable, insulting, insufferable,
injurious, iniquitous, inexcusable, inappropriate,
impish, iffy, icky, hostile, horrid, horrible, hideous,
heinous, gruesome, grisly, ghoulish, ghastly, frightful,
(Susie, such a wretched heap of trochees!),
foul, fishy, evil, dreadful, distressing, disreputable,

dismal, devious, despicable, depraved, deleterious,
debauched, dastardly, culpable, crooked, creepy,
contemptible, chilling, blasphemous, base, atrocious,
appalling, alarming, abysmal, abusive, and abominable.
Ahem. But I dare not squash.
The governing principle of the cosmos
might be some bleak spidery karma—
some insufferable Kafkaesque
labyrinthine vorticular cauldron
(cauldronic vortex?) of god-
awful misery—and I prefer not (O Bartleby)
to be on the wrong end of a trillion
fangs, trillions of spidery legs....
Soon I'll be back in the Yucatán:
getting nibbled by 'sea ants' (tiny reef-
guarding jellyfish, Susie—what a planet!),
diving *cenotes,* and swigging tequila
intravenously, amen.
Spiders in the Yucatán shall not be juggled
with, either. Example: last winter, in the jungled
ruins at Coba, one chomped my brother—
poor Mark, his ankle ballooning
with the welts of dengue fever,
or whatever poison those beasties carry
upon their terrible lips, if spiders have lips.
But Mark is not done with his suffering:
he has bought Big Ben a fire truck, what Mark
at Ben's age called a *fy-ray-ray.* When I crawl
back up the icy hill—fatter, more grizzled,
windswept to microscopic shreds—I'll drizzle

some Cragganmore over ice, giggle
at the irony. I'll try and fail to teach
Ben C-major on the piano. His only wish
is to pummel the three dozen alarming
noise buttons on his new fire truck.
Some toy chateau must be ablaze!
This house, Susie, is Babylon.
Perhaps the pantheon of capricious and irritable
gods will again curse humanity
for its intolerable clamor, and Orgeval—
and every sleepy village and raucous metropolis
across the globe—will by New Years be undersea
tombs, minarets and skyscrapers and steeples
and radio towers and space needles
and the Great God-Damned Wall of China
all jutting from the sea floor like the masts
of innumerable ancient vessels
that today litter the Adriatic, the Aegean, the Ionian—
O epic cemetery that is the Mediterranean.
Yea, every creeping thing that creepeth
upon the Earth will have fucking drowned-eth.
Curses, what a lousy Yuletide sentiment!
Fuck it, I'm not Bing Crosby.
To thwart the impending watery Apocalypse,
we've planned a grisly sacrifice to the gods
(poor Uncle Mark), so it's shaping up
after all to be a holly-jolly X-mas.
All the icebergs arrive on schedule
and, Ho Ho Ho, the cabinet is full of scotch.
My French lexicon swells by atomic degrees, la la la.

Ben knows, in two languages, where Santa is: *voilà,*
at the ceiling, bobbing his helium bob.
That boy is a prize. And the planet,
Susie—lover of maps and of words,
lovely spinner of the tired,
tired world—dammit all to hell, Susie Meserve,
the planet shall be saved.

Letter to Self at 22 from 35

It's good to hear from you, Jackass,
via your sad little self-published tirades,
bound at a local print shop in Albany,
New York. I found them in the rusty belly
of a file cabinet. I had to shoo away
a diabolical spider no doubt pissing
on your poems, though spiders don't pee
the way we do (do they?), and I'm still
sneezing from thirteen years of dust.
The museum of one's self is an eerie place:
one doesn't recognize the fossils,
and no convenient map hangs on the wall
of a Great Hall. Look: my old community
college ID cards. And here: my nametag
from that god-forsaken pharmacy—
I don't know how you suffer the miserable
coupon-clipping geezers (cliché #1),
the spine-bending hours, the interminable
shelves of newspapers and floss and pain
relievers and vitamins, the cold razor
of 6 AM.... Numbskull, how lucky I am
to have stumbled upon these hieroglyphs
of my own history, these beer-soaked
scribbles that are pulling you through
the eyes of innumerable needles—needles
as thin as you, but not as thin as your sad
little bank account, and more terrible.
Those two dimes still rattle the same
sickening, sickening, sickening rattle.
Poor-ass crappy poet, can you hear the dime-

rattle of the word *sickening*? I'm sorry
to tell you that those dimes are not as shiny,
and they're worth less. Listen, Shakespeare,
your faux-philosophical rants are not bound
for the Smithsonian. What the hell you are
thinking (cliché #2) remains elusive.
You should hop yourself up (cliché #3)
on something deeper and wiser than beer.
The eyeballs of your poems seep with it.
Ha ha, what has changed! Nevertheless,
Knuckle Head, I know more than you.
Example: you will teach creative writing—
O merciless, unspeakable, migraine irony....
Sour dropout, your days of stockboy drudgery
are not over, O cornucopia of warehouse
hangovers. Grouchy Bukowski fan, your city
will be bombed. Crybaby, your muse will fall
off the face of the Earth (cliché #4), goodbye
and goodbye to Katie, you fucking crybaby.
Cheer up, Columbus: soon you will explore
the green Caribbean—your college days sailing
behind, your majestic flags of empire billowing.
You will not be forever stuck in the abyss
of that Albany flat: your landlord with her fat,
sweaty arms screaming, screaming for the rent
because the world has failed you both,
your roommates screeching their intolerable
screech from atop a collapsing skyscraper
of utility bills, and that sense of hopelessness
so familiar you call it 'Bill.' Well, no more.

Sad little Kerouacian hobo, I'm green with envy
(cliché #5—my god, that one is wretched)—
the rest of your life ahead of you (cliché #6—
will this ever end? (cliché #7—shoot me!
(cliché #8—one more and I'll self-combust
(cliché #9)))). [Pause for self-combustion.]
These clichés are for you, Dummy—ogre
of the unoriginal, mopey maestro of mixed
metaphor, heartless tyrant of the intangible,
bully of bewildering syntax, czar of craftless
crap.... But, Idiot Inkster, you couldn't know
what I know. And if you could, you would
loop a helix around the starry Christmas tree
of your gloom, and only Death could unravel you.
Cheer up, cheerless chump: other luminous
things are taking form in the cosmic goo.
Example: though he won't arrive for a decade,
your nephew unravels toward you, a string
dangling from a universe of potential, amen.
His mother will traverse the globe, Paris
to San Francisco, stumble into your wide-eyed
brother in a taxicab, and that's when Big Ben
will begin to knock on the door of this world.
Can you hear him? At 2, he's a spinning nucleus
of energy, a cyclone of joy, a tiny Big Bang.
Nothing like you, Sir Pessimism, Señor Sulk.
You should be more like your brother, spending
his lunch breaks passing out free poems
to the goons of Market Street—corporate goons
wailing intolerable corporate songs, bending

their corporate spines to the spineless,
pitiless gods of the American Work Ethic,
and your brother saying *fuck that,* saying *free*
poem, saying *genesis,* saying *here,* and watching
his words scatter like confetti over San Francisco
as though a war had ended—the heroes waving
from convertibles sailing the narrow avenues,
the marching band in tatters, the distant cities
bubbling heroically under tremendous infernos—
and maybe the war had been a personal war,
and your brother—daddy to that dynamo
nephew of yours—not an ounce of darkness
in his spine, standing tall and defiant on Market
Street, a lost muse, a lost saint, maybe Saint Valentine,
as the corporate goons limp back to their heartless
caves, their thrumming hives of ignorance....
Spineless dullard, why are you thus incapable?
Instead, capital-D Dunce, you spiral away
into the vortex of your own stockboy misery,
huddled in your darkened, cluttered room cursing
the alarming numbers tumbling daily into your
sad mailbox, cursing protons for their positive
charge, and composing a library of dreadful poems
which, despite a decade of training, I cannot
decipher. I'm flummoxed: what is the shadow
of the sky? What is the dust of dreams, and why
is it chasing canyons? Never mind. My room
is still a tempestuous typhoon of useless papers.
I still lament, lament, lament. The skyscrapers
of unpaid bills will never stop collapsing

into tiresome rubble. My ambition's a bird,
la la la. My darling is still the elegy, the tolling
bell, of last call. O my sweet old et cetera....
But don't curse the proton. The proton,
Mikey, is a tremendous, tremendous thing.

Letter to So-and-So from Wherever

Hey, what you said to me was inappropriate—
explicit graffiti scrawled on a temple wall
barked as slam poetry at the funeral
of an orphaned 9-year-old leukemia victim....
But perhaps you're not to blame—
lately I've been intolerant of everything:
my empty, empty mailbox,
the voiceless planets, even my own skeleton,
whose grin I find galling.
I've considered punching out my own teeth
and mailing them to you—your city
which has never been bombed.
It's chilly here, not that you care
where I am, or how chaos theory gurgles
in my kitchen sink—how the rickety towers
of plates could crush me. You couldn't
imagine where I am
if I shoved a globe down your throat
and the globe settled in your womb
and next spring you gave birth to a geography whiz....
Hint: no coconut trees, no igloos.
Hint: interstates strung like attic cobwebs
between the city's poles.
I'm somewhere in the middle, a place
as middling and boring as you found me—
my disinterest in eco-feminism,
in sweaty bus rides to the Capitol,
in vegan tirades, in weed.
I want to call you the hippest
dirty names, but I've been idling

in a non-specific mood.
The good news is, I kind of like this
non-specific glowering in your direction.
The bad news is, it's moral–
I mean as a dilemma–
to ask my students to knock off
their bloody over-generalizing.
Their sleepy spittle will be the end of civilization!
Their children will be little amorphous blobs!
But gin-soaked at noon,
I told them what you said to me,
and they gasped, so I gave them all A's.
Their collective gasp sounded like atoms
splitting, but without the mushroom cloud and fire
and shadows blasted into temple walls.
There are no temple walls here,
despite the many temples.
I can't explain how this works,
but I can't explain lots of things:
how your cat will live to be 100
like my senile, broken-hipped great-grandmother,
how vowels drop like pinballs
from your flapping tongue, drop
straight through the Earth. . . .
I turned what you said to me into haiku.
Having no pastoral Japanese river handy,
I floated them along a gutter
pregnant with rainwater.
I turned what you said to me into origami
sparrows, then crumpled them

because they were too specific,
and in that crumpling I heard your voice—
like a bird's, wings crushed—whistling
above my crumpled, crumpled city.

Letter to Sanders from Academia

Daniel, my mom would love you
to say 'Academia'—almost
as much as she loves me to mutter
that bloated pasty-faced turtle-necked
Xerox-choked word. Sorry, got something stuck
in my throat: icicles of glass, or strychnine....
Ahem. Keep things in perspective, young Jedi:
survive you will.
Last I heard from you, you were sailing
the dark ship of Corporate America.
Well, 'sailing' suggests captainhood—
let's say you were a galley slave,
one in an infinite hive
of galley slaves, all of you emaciated, an inch
from the flat rim of the Earth.
Such sharp edges in this world....
In your desperate cable, all the old images
were in place: sporty ties like a flock
of pigeons splattering every cubicle,
the water in the cooler darkened
by the silt of senseless chatter, all the clocks
spinning in reverse like drunk hurricanes,
galaxies tanked on gin and stumbling home—
back to some zero-hour, some
timeless cradle.... And the epic
tragedy: poetry
thinning from your blood, your plasma
gasping for freedom from a cage
crafted not from iron but from paper clips—
more bendable than what a paper clip symbolizes,

i.e. conform or suffer, i.e. say goodbye
to your useless amorous creative impulses,
your squashed *duende.*
O College Graduate, O Spanish Major,
be Romantic and translate it: *adios, duende....*
But you're not alone, so don't bend
under the skyscraper weight of your despair.
Be careful—you've seen what can happen
to a skyscraper, and Superman
is dead. Like Hugo,
I'm using too many r's, but how else to spell
rrrrrrrr?
Don't worry: my brother, a creative genius,
has survived in your shoes for a decade plus.
Then again, as his wife's belly swells
for the second time, I worry
that she'll finally give birth
to a little tie. How would they dress it
for graduations, weddings, funerals?
Or, jumping Jesus, for job interviews?
My brother and I still plan to burn
our ties—both literal and abstract—
on some beach far away from the Things of Man.
We practiced once: in a suburban barbecue pit
we grilled some ties, watched the pollution
rise over the backyard redwood, over Walnut Creek,
over Mount Diablo, over the Bay, over America,
over the god-damned Milky Way—
O our polluted lives....
Consider me, Daniel: the illustrious Mike Dockins!

Some days I wish we could trade places.
Example: days when even a poor skater could skate
flawless eights across the pond
of my students' eyeballs, my own pupils dismal.
Example: days when I suffer paper cuts
on my fucking brain, paper cuts
across each mitochondrion and Golgi apparatus,
my messenger-RNA leaping cellular miles
toward some cytoplasmic Marathon
only to collapse in a microscopic heap
muttering sour news.
Example: days when my paycheck weighs
less than my saltine lunch, less than a molecule
of NaCl on that flimsy cracker....
Daniel, I bet you make more money than me,
you magnificent bastard,
not that either of us are driven
by *kapital,* or are troubled by the mysterious
red and blue fibers wriggling
like worms in the hearts of dollar bills.
But money, some say, makes the world
go round (not, you know, cosmic inertia).
But say you're in a tin can
orbiting Titan and you've got a $50 bill
and no groceries: you're fucked.
O Titan, little foreign moon-planet.
O far-flung eyeball. O contingency plan
for when we incinerate the Earth.
O retirement home to my little corporate niece,
my darling tie of a nephew.

Titan Titan Titan Titan Titan....
I feel better already. But who else
gives a flying orbital fuck about the Space
Program, about Science? So let's get back,
Daniel, to what people care about: misery.
Example: silence at the end of the day.
Example: wolves at the end of the month.
My wolves are paper wolves:
paper jaws, paper gullets, and worst,
a paper hunger. 'Come save me,'
you gurgled in your desperate wire.
But—you magnificent bastard, you terrific bum,
you poor, skinny, talented ragamuffin—
what about me? Crap,
I can see the credits from here, though I curse
my astigmatism and I don't know what *here* is.
The 3 o'clock bell tolls: for us, for us, for us.
Pug-faced urchins with anxious knuckles
pound fists into meaty palms
as though typing a single letter
over and over: o, o, o, o, o....
The schoolyard will soon be a cemetery.
Santa Claus, stalked by wolves
(yes, even Santa), lugs an empty sack
to his icy bungalow, and the wretched island
of misfit toys sinks into the Arctic—
goodbye raggedy dolly with one eye
(O cataclysmic, cycloptic dolly),
goodbye wheel-less choo-choo—
and somehow it's all very jolly.

A ruined girl, some Sylvia, spills
her last glass of milk,
flings her final lullaby into the Void.
Something in Denmark is rotten, rotten, rotten.
I know what that something is,
and I got an A, and I don't fucking care
if that A is scarlet: the answer is rottenness.
Poor Phoebe Caulfield: the word *fuck*
scrawled like galactic collisions across her
ignorant school walls, and who the fuck cares
about the collisions of galaxies?
Her poor big brother: his lousy lousyness,
his crummy crummyness,
graying, like all of us,
at 16. Poor Gatsby: face-down in the pool,
snorkeling the reef of Death, a hole
in his belly shaped like the rotten American
Dream. Poor Humbert: his lust crumpled
(interstate motels, depravity), his vision
blurred by haze—goodbye Dolly—
fires slug after slug into the flapping,
unflappable Q.
Poor flappable All of Us: the forlorn rags
of growing old, the end of the Road....
The Dean has dissolved, and Paradise slouches
on the old broken-down river pier,
watching the long, long skies over New Jersey,
and don't you know, Daniel,
that God is Pooh Bear? Hallelujah,
it's Exodus: all are walking away from Omelas,

the grim mop friendless at last.
The peg-legged captain trembles
at the harpoon line, and epic Leviathan,
pulling the captain down down down, sounds
to the bottom of the ocean—a classic
fusion of cetology and transcendentalism.
I wish I could unlearn. Gilgamesh
loses Paradise to his exhaustion, and the serpent
sounds to the very bottom of the Infinite,
that perfect and waterless abyss. . . .
The slanted blade of the guillotine
falls and falls toward the core of the Earth—
O Newtonian violence, O interminable physics.
Don't you see what's happening?
The Big Bang has exhausted itself—
it's run out of space!—and now the cosmos,
in a staggering whip lash of physics and irony,
catapults back toward the insufferable
singularity, that dismal speck
whence the origin of all things, the whole
enormous sadness of all things.
(Kerouac: for you, another despicable nickel.
I'm running out of nickels. I hope it rattles
your skeleton like a Salt Lake jukebox). Daniel,
don't panic: the Big Crunch won't happen
for like 13.7 eons, or something
equally nerdy, amen.
Meantime, Titan is our last hope:
this moon may be an uninhabitable deathscape,
but it's got ice and volcanoes,

maybe a few trillion plate-tectonic
microbial critters spewing microbial gripes
from the rims of trench vents
(think of their rants!),
and, who knows, maybe there's a grove
of clementine trees,
a clean and well-lighted saloon,
a divine haze—divine smog, even—
from the glorious, glorious blaze of ties.
Yes, Daniel, our inferno will not ignore
even the microbial, the leptonic. We need
a small, good thing
in a time like this when we're mourning
the loss of fill-in-the-blank
and fill-in-the-blank and fill-in-the-blank....
Fuck it.
I'll see you soon, Pal, in the belly
of the wolf, and, god-dammit all to hell,
we'll sing to Titan as we dissolve. At last,
a happy ending.

Acknowledgments

I would like to express my deep gratitude to Santa Claus, Travis Denton, Robyn Art, Audrey Johnston, Allison Jenks, Beth Gylys, Tony Moon, English 101, Michelle Bonczek Evory, Maureen Seaton, Nina Ellen Riggs, James Wright, Benjamin Dockins, Jamie Iredell, Li Po, Susie Meserve, Self at 22, So-and-So, and Daniel Sanders, for being sports.

To my family—Dad, Mom, Matt, Mark, Gwen, Benjamin, & Gabriel—for letting me stomp around in the business of words.

To Michelle Bonczek Evory, Beth Gylys, Meg Harper, Tom Holmes, Sara Bartlett Large, Josh Russell, and especially Jamie Iredell, for invaluable feedback on early drafts of this collection.

To William Heyen, for telling me to 'get involved in something long.'

To Vickery's in Midtown Atlanta (& to Josh Brewer, Cathy Davidson, Christi Gregor, Tony Moon, Rose Lester Poland, Katie Sears, Beth Wright, and everyone else), for being my second home during the drafting & revising of many of these poems, not to mention for all the PBRs.

To Richard Hugo, of course.

To Jack Kerouac & Charles Bukowski, for being honest.

I am grateful to the editors of the following journals, in which many of the poems in this book were originally published, sometimes in different forms:

Atticus Review: 'Letter to Jenks from Hurricane Jeanne'

Lamination Colony: 'Letter to So-and-So from Wherever'

Meat For Tea: 'Letter to Denton from O'Hare'

The National Poetry Review: 'Letter to Bonczek from Brockport'

New South (formerly *GSU Review*): 'Letter to Sanders from Academia'

Night Hawk Review: 'Letter to Seaton from a Little Ice Age'

Pank: 'Letter to Iredell from the Yucatán'

Poetry Midwest: 'Letter to Gylys from Midtown,' 'Letter to Moon from Luquillo' and 'Letter to Riggs from Cobble Hill'

Santa Clara Review: 'Letter to Art from Greenwich'

Scythe: 'Letter to Dockins from a Foreign Country,' 'Letter to Li Po from Vickery's' and 'Letter to Self at 22 from 35'

Sub-Lit: 'Letter to English 101 from the South Fucking Pole'

Third Coast: 'Letter to Johnston from Carlisle' and 'Letter to Jenks from Hurricane Ivan'

West Branch: 'Letter to Claus from Walnut Creek'

Mike Dockins was born in 1972 and grew up in Yonkers, New York. He holds a BS from SUNY Brockport (1999), an MFA from the University of Massachusetts Amherst (2002), and a PHD from Georgia State University (2010). His poems have appeared in *Crazyhorse, The Gettysburg Review, Quarterly West, Willow Springs, Salt Hill, Indiana Review, Gulf Coast, jubilat, The Offending Adam, Atlanta Review,* and elsewhere, and they have been reprinted on *Poetry Daily, Verse Daily,* and in the 2007 edition of *The Best American Poetry.* His critically-acclaimed first book of poems, *Slouching in the Path of a Comet* (Sage Hill Press, 2007), after moving 850 copies, is currently anticipating a third print run. *Letter to So-and-So from Wherever,* his second collection, was a co-winner of the first annual Maxine Kumin Prize in Poetry. Mike moonlights as a singer-songwriter. *Fame For Zoe,* the latest full-length album from his acoustic-pop duo Clop, is available on iTunes. For the last 14 summers, he has taught creative writing in Johns Hopkins University's Center for Talented Youth summer program at its Dickinson College campus in Carlisle, Pennsylvania.

The Maxine Kumin Prize in Poetry

MAXINE KUMIN came to prominence as one of a generation of women poets who extended the boundaries of poetry, addressing areas of female experience which had not previously been written about. A Pulitzer Prize-winning poet, her spare, deceptively simple lines explored some of the most complex aspects of human existence—birth and death, evanescence and renewal, and the events large and small conjoining them all. An enduring presence in American poetry, Maxine Kumin's career spanned over half a century. She was the recipient of prestigious awards such as the Pulitzer Prize, the Ruth Lilly Poetry Prize, and an American Academy and Institute of Arts and Letters Award. She was the poetry consultant for the Library of Congress in 1981–1982, and taught at many of the country's most prestigious universities, including Massachusetts Institute of Technology, Princeton, and Columbia. She was a frequent faculty member at the Bread Loaf Writers' Conference and a beloved mentor & friend to younger poets & writers. She lived in Warner, New Hampshire and died in 2014. The Maxine Kumin Prize in Poetry is a tribute developed during C&R Press's first open poetry reading period in December 2013 during the last weeks of her life.

www.ingramcontent.com/pod-product-compliance
Lightning Source LLC
Chambersburg PA
CBHW021014090426
42738CB00007B/778